THE UNIVERSITY OF MICHIGAN
CENTER FOR CHINESE STUDIES

MICHIGAN PAPERS IN CHINESE STUDIES
NO. 35

DOUBLE JEOPARDY
A CRITIQUE OF SEVEN YÜAN COURTROOM DRAMAS

by
Ching-Hsi Perng

Ann Arbor

Center for Chinese Studies
The University of Michigan

1978

Open access edition funded by the National Endowment for the Humanities/ Andrew W. Mellon Foundation Humanities Open Book Program.

Library of Congress Cataloging in Publication Data

Perng, Ching-Hsi.
  Double Jeopardy.

  (Michigan papers in Chinese studies; no. 35)
  Bibliography: p.
  1. Chinese drama--Yüan dynasty, 1260-1368--History and criticism. 2. Trials--China--Drama. I. Title. II. Series.

PL2384.P4   895.1'2'4093   78-13029
ISBN 978-0-89-264035-5

Printed and bound by CPI Group (UK) Ltd, Croydon, CR0 4YY

ISBN 978-0-89-264035-5 (hardcover)
ISBN 978-0-47-203799-5 (paper)
ISBN 978-0-47-212737-5 (ebook)
ISBN 978-0-47-290132-6 (open access)

for Jim

for Jim

CONTENTS

viii

PREFACE

Traditionally, criticism of Yüan drama has been dominated by the "poetic" and the "socialist" schools. The present work represents a rather rigorous attempt to evaluate a group of plays by aesthetic criteria generated from within the genre itself. Seven "judgment reversal" plays constitute the body of this work, and its two major preoccupations are language and the manipulation of dramatic characters-- undoubtedly the most reliable indicators of the playwright's strength and craftsmanship in such a stylized art form as Yüan tsa-chü drama.

The method informing the present volume is basically just explication de texte, with particular attention to both the conventions of the genre and the individual characters of each play. Close scrutiny of some conventional aspects of tsa-chü--the functions of lyric, verse, and prose and the significance of their distribution in the play; the custom of a single singing role and its implication for the presentation of dramatis personae, and so on--will reveal the innovation and creative vitality of the playwright. Even though I deal with a small subgroup within the genre, Yüan drama being as convention-bound as it is, I believe some of the methods used and values adduced will be applicable to Yüan dramatic criticism as a whole.

During the preparation of this book I became indebted to many people. Special thanks go to all members of my dissertation com- mittee--Professors Russell A. Fraser, Shuen-fu Lin, William F. Sibley, and Charles Witke--for their advice and constant encouragement.

To Professor J. I. Crump, chairman of the committee, I would like to express my deepest gratitude. Not only did his erudition on the subject help me greatly with my task, but when aid or inspiration was needed he was always there, ready. His imprint must be apparent on every page; but that, I hope, is the least that I have gained from a very special person.

x

Professor Lin, a particularly attentive reader, furnished perceptive and constructive criticism. Professor Stephen H. West, of the University of Arizona, read the second chapter in its earlier version, and kindly offered many valuable comments and suggestions.

In addition, I am grateful to have this small forum from which to acknowledge publicly my sincere thanks to Professors Charles Witke and Ilene Olken, Directors of the Program in Comparative Literature at The University of Michigan, who over the years have graciously and staunchly supported my various projects. I would also like to acknowledge my debt to the Center for Chinese Studies at The University of Michigan for making me an associate so I could continue to work on this book.

But nothing I can say here will adequately repay my debt to my dear parents and my beloved wife. Their unstinted moral support, patience, and love have made this work possible, for whatever it may be worth.

C. H. P.

ABBREVIATIONS

CW   Chung-wen ta tz'u-tien 中文大辭典

KTHC   Chung-kuo ku-tien hsi-ch'ü lun-chu chi-ch'eng 中國古典戲曲論著集成

WP   Yüan-ch'ü hsüan wai-pien 元曲選外編

YCH   Yüan-ch'ü hsüan 元曲選

YMC   Yüan-Ming-Ch'ing hsi-ch'ü lun-wen chi 元明清戲曲論文集

I. PRELIMINARIES

This study examines and evaluates a group of seven plays from the Yüan Dynasty (1260-1368) tsa-chü drama 雜劇 known as "p'ing-fan kung-an chü 平反公案劇 [1] or "plays of judgment reversal," all of which feature double trials in which the verdict of the first judge is overturned by that of the second. In the sense that these plays constitute a distinct group within the subgenre of kung-an chü 公案劇 or "courtroom plays," the present project is an extension of Professor George A. Hayden's recent work.[2] What do these plays have in common beyond the obvious fact that they all include double trials? In what way is the first verdict arrived at, and how does the second come about? What bearing does such an arrangement have on the dramas' structure or the manipulation of characters? Further, how are these structurally and often thematically similar plays different from one another? These are some of the questions that will be dealt with in the following chapters.

But the study goes further. Less broad in scope than Hayden's paper,[3] it can afford discussion in more detail and accommodate a more rigorous aesthetic analysis with a certain degree of thoroughness. While theme and structure are touched upon, the present investigation concentrates in particular on the dramatic uses of language and the maneuvering of dramatis personae. For it is in these last two areas, I believe, that the Yüan playwright's art is revealed. Questions will be raised about the proportion of poetic arias to prose dialogue in these plays as compared to other tsa-chü. What, for instance, does their distribution tell us about the nature of the judgment reversal dramas as opposed to other kinds of Yüan plays?[4] Specifically, what function does spoken verse (and recapitulations) have in a dramatic situation? Are there patterns or conventions in characterization? What is the relationship between the custom of a single singing role and the presentation of characters? Finally, what is the implication of the reversal of judgment? Does it, however obliquely, point to the Chinese sense of the "tragic" or reflect to any degree Chinese sensibilities?

1

It is obvious that such an endeavor will necessarily go well beyond explication de texte for a handful of plays, if only to do justice to the significance of the questions raised. By taking up the present research, I hope to bring into sharper focus criteria for the evaluation not only of the plays under scrutiny but also of the Yüan tsa-chü as a dramatic form. In the process of comparing and contrasting plays with structural and thematic similarities, I hope standards will appear for judging the use of language and the manipulation of characters in most Yüan plays. More importantly, these standards will have been generated from the works themselves: they will not be alien rules imposed on the works from without. Moreover, since the establishment of such a set of criteria might mark the end of dilettantish "appreciation" and the beginning of serious criticism, the effort has a worthy goal. This is not mere wishful thinking; given the fact that Yüan drama is a highly stylized and conventionalized art form, the plays of judgment reversal have much in common with other groups or subgenres of tsa-chü. In many cases findings here may be directly applicable to the rest of the genre; in others, some modification should make them useful. At any rate, with caution and judiciousness, this study can be used as a basis upon which a larger framework of criticism of Yüan drama may be built. The argument boils down to this: while the proximate target of the present research is seven plays of judgment reversal, its ultimate end is a better critical understanding of the tsa-chü as a genre.

Of the 161 extant Yüan dramas,[5] 7 belong to the group of "judgment reversal" plays. They are determined as such on the basis of the following criteria: 1) there must be at least two trials, both of which are presented on stage; 2) the verdict of the first judge must be overruled by that of the second; and 3) the reversal or the process of reversal must constitute the play's focal point of interest. These strictures leave us with the following plays:[6]

1) The Child Shen-nu-erh (Shen-nu-erh 神奴兒), anon.[7]

2) Judgment on the Kerchief (K'an t'ou-chin 勘頭巾), by Lu Teng-shan 陸登善 .

3) Rescue of a Filial Son (Chiu hsiao-tze 救孝子),[8] by Wang Chung-wen 王仲文 .

4) The Chalk Circle (Hui-lan chi 灰闌記), by Li Hsing-tao 李行道 .

5) The Mo-ho-lo Doll (Mo-ho-lo 魔合羅), by Meng Han-ch'ing 孟漢卿·

6) Injustice to Tou Ngo (Tou Ngo yüan 竇娥寃), by Kuan Han-ch'ing 關漢卿·

7) The Gold Phoenix Hairpins (Chin feng ch'ai 金鳳釵), by Cheng T'ing-yü 鄭廷玉·

Revelation in a Dream (Fei yi ming 緋衣夢) and The Butterfly Dream (Hu-tieh meng 蝴蝶夢), both attributed to Kuan Han-ch'ing, have been excluded because in each case the first trial transpires between the acts and is simply reported. The Yen-an Court (Yen-an fu 延安府)[9] appears to be another judgment reversal drama, but there is in fact only one verdict given during the entire play.

A few words must be said about The Mo-ho-lo Doll. Some scholars believe that the judge of the first trial also presides over the second trial,[10] but the Yüan text upon which the theory is based is, to begin with, too truncated to be a reliable source in itself. (More on this when we take up the problem of texts.) The circumstances surrounding this drama and its two court scenes are ambiguous at best and subject to different interpretations. Besides, though a clerk, Chang Ting (as in another play, Judgment on the Kerchief) assumes the role of a de facto magistrate in the review trial and he deserves to be treated as the second judge.

The miscarriage of justice in The Gold Phoenix Hairpins and The Child Shen-nu-erh takes place relatively late (in the third act), but in both instances the treatment of the courtroom scenes as well as the ensuing review trial warrants their inclusion in our group. All the other plays set the initial trial in the second act and the review trial in the fourth and last act. (Judgment on the Kerchief is the only exception: its review trial comes in the third act, making the final act perfunctorily anticlimactic as far as dramatic structure is concerned.) In any event, the commission of the crime--always murder in cold blood--occurs earlier on in the play, and soon after the erroneous court decision is made the search for the true culprits and the redressing of the wrongs become the motives for the remaining action. Thus these plays, to varying degrees, become "detective stories."[11]

While the seven plays constitute the corpus of our investigation, references to other tsa-chü is both inevitable and desirable. Where necessary, they, too, will be discussed at length. For example, to pinpoint the characteristic use of language in the plays of judgment reversal, which are plot oriented, illustrations from such "poetic" dramas as Autumn in the Palace of Han (Han-kung ch'iu 漢宮秋) or Rain on the Wu-t'ung Trees (Wu-t'ung yü 梧桐雨) form illuminating contrasts. Or, in the study of conventional characters (an innkeeper, say), information provided by plays outside of our select group can furnish useful background against which the playwright's handling of his dramatis personae may be evaluated.

A Historical Survey of Criticism

I have alluded to the desirability of establishing certain critical standards for the evaluation of Yüan drama, so it is incumbent upon me to give a brief history of tsa-chü criticism to orient the reader. Traditionally, tsa-chü criticism in China has been characterized by two strong tendencies: one is to view these plays not as drama but as poetry; the other is to consider them literature of protest. These two tendencies are not mutually exclusive and may be manifested in the same critic. In addition to these indigenous "schools," there has been more recently vigorous critical attention sprouting in foreign soil.

The "Poetic" School

Critics of this school are preoccupied almost solely with the poetic quality of tsa-chü. Their interest lies in the arias of a play, for which they have laid down meticulous rules both descriptive and prescriptive. They have consigned the dramatic and theatrical elements of tsa-chü to oblivion when in fact those elements account for much--if not all--of the genre's success and popularity as the theater of the period.

The major critical work by a contemporary of the Yüan playwrights themselves says nothing about tsa-chü as drama: Chou Te-ch'ing's 周 德清 Chung-yüan yin-yün 中原音韻 [Rhymes of the Central Plain] (1324)[12] concerns itself entirely with poetics and prosody. The book's professed aim is to promote "correct diction and elevated style";[13] it achieves just that and no more. The pamphlet "Ch'ang lun" 唱論 [On Singing],[14] by an anonymous Yüan writer who chose to style himself Yen-nan Chih-an 燕南芝菴, remains the only extant Yüan document on the art of singing in a tsa-chü performance. It is still disappointing, however, because it does not deal so much with singing as with the various rhyming systems in songs. It is another "poet's primer" with a misleading title. And from what we can ascertain today, the pamphlet's statements on the thematic implication of the modal arrangement of music can only be accepted with a grain of salt.[15]

The dramatic aspects of tsa-chü continued to be neglected by the Ming critics, who apparently inherited their predecessors' predilection for poetry. T'ai-ho cheng-yin p'u 太和正音譜 [Formularies of Supreme Harmony] (1398),[16] by Chu Ch'üan 朱權, that talented prince-turned-playwright-critic, is an important contribution to the study of tsa-chü, being the first to assess the achievement of Yüan masters. But the main thrust of the book again resides in Chu's meticulous--and sometimes embarrassingly frivolous--effort to provide "correct" prosodic formulae for most of the established song sets, complete with injunctions on the determination of tones. The importance of poetry (which is often equated with music) is blown so out of proportion that the dramatic side of tsa-chü has received far less attention than its due. Small wonder that Kuan Han-ch'ing, recognized nowadays as one of China's greatest playwrights, is hardly Chu Ch'üan's favorite. When he includes Kuan in his list of "talented song writers, past and present," Chu feels compelled to apologize, as if for a lapse in taste:

觀其詞語. 乃可上可下之才. 蓋所以取者.
初為雜劇之始, 故卓以前列.

To judge from [Kuan's] language, he has the potential to be good but also can be bad. [Or, ". . . his talent is a border-line case between the upper (superior) and the lower (infe-rior)."] Indeed, it is only because the tsa-chü genre started with the man that he is [here] ranked so high.[17]

Consequently, Chu's criticism is of value to the student of drama on two counts: it is the first to classify tsa-chü into twelve categories; for even though the classification is quite arbitrary and without elabora-tion or illustration it is a form of evaluation. Secondly, Chu's work contains notes, albeit sketchy ones, on a dozen or so tsa-chü terms. One wishes that Chu had concentrated and done a more thorough job in those two areas.

Wang Chi-te's 王驥德 Ch'ü lü 曲律,[18] published in 1624, is probably the most extensive and informative work on the art of tsa-chü to have come from a Ming scholar-critic. The scope of the book's forty sections, divided unevenly into four chapters, ranges from general discussions on the origin of ch'ü to the more specific, such as the vice of using "incorrect" words. But again, its emphasis is on the musical and poetic components, and the work remains largely what its title indicates: Rules for Arias. From time to time throughout the book, however, Wang does bring up topics of dramatic import (for instance, the function and significance of comic interludes [ch'a-k'o 插科]), thus kindling in the reader who is keen on drama hopes which are soon dashed, for even in the few places that he discusses dramatic matters, a skimpy treatment is about all Wang manages to furnish.[19]

Another Ming work worthy of mention is Shen Te-fu's 沈德符 Ku-ch'ü tsa-yen 顧曲雜言 [Miscellaneous Remarks on Tsa-chü] (1618).[20] Brief but influential, it offers views not merely on the musical/poetic aspects of tsa-chü, but on instruments and dancing as well, making it a more balanced critical work than either Chu Ch'üan's T'ai-ho cheng-yin p'u or Wang Chi-te's Ch'ü lü. But as criticism of drama (which to be honest it does not claim to be), it leaves a lot to be desired.

Besides being indifferent drama critics, some Ming scholars are also notorious spawners of incorrect information. Even Wang and Shen are no exceptions. It was Shen, for instance, who first suggested that the composition of dramatic verse was required in Yüan Dynasty civil service examinations.[21] Preposterous as the theory was, it nevertheless gained great currency among later Chinese literati. The best evidence of Shen's influence is in the case of Tsang Mao-hsün. The eminent compiler of Yüan-chü hsüan 元曲選 (YCH) [An Anthology of Yüan Drama] subscribes to Shen's theory in one of his prefaces to the anthology.[22] Wang Chi-te, on his part, advanced another theory cut from whole cloth. He declared that the arias and prose dialogue in any particular Yüan play were done by different hands:

> The arias in Yüan drama are all excellent as lyric, but the dialogue is generally rustic and obscene and does not sound [as though it comes from] literati. This is because in those days the dialogue was first set up by the musicians of the drama school and then the designated poets composed the arias, [a practice] called "filling in the lyrics." What the musicians had written, the literati would not deign to correct. Hence the plot [of Yüan drama] is often against the law of nature, and the diction largely incomprehensible.[23]

Both Shen's and Wang's views have long since been relegated to
their proper place--pastures filled with chimeras and laughing stock
created by less sensible and more daring critics. But one must not
lose sight of their serious implications. In advancing their theories,
Shen and Wang extolled arias over prose dialogue, and poet-playwright
over mere musician or player. It is not totally inconceivable that the
misrepresentation of historical facts was deliberate on the part of
Chinese scholars in whom the love for poetry was sovereign. The cases
of Shen and Wang largely reflect the literati's concern and predilection
for poetry--even when faced with a genre plainly intended for the theater.
Such concerns and predilections are in turn manifested in their criticism.
It is certainly no coincidence that most Chinese critics used the term
ch'ü 曲 (aria or song) for tsa-chü when the more comprehensive and
exact term hsi-ch'ü (drama and song, or dramatic song) existed.
Granted, it may be argued that ch'ü, in its broader sense, denoted both
drama and song, but the content of the critical works cited above more
than indicates that the narrower sense was adopted by critics of the day.
The ambiguous use of the term seems to have been intentional: one is
tempted to see in it a conspiracy of Chinese literati to turn a dramatic
form into yet another poetic medium.[24]

Thus, Chinese dramatic criticism continued to be marked by the
conspicuous absence of a sensible and balanced critic--until Li Yü 李漁
(1611-1676). A prolific writer, Li was the author of sixteen plays in
the ch'uan-ch'i 傳奇 style, most of which were met with enthusiastic
response.[25] His greatest contribution to Chinese theater, however, lies
in the monumental work on dramaturgy contained in the five-volume
Hsien-ch'ing ou-chi 閑情偶記 [Occasional Notes at Leisure] (1671).[26]
A listing of the work's relevant contents makes it plain as to how he
parted company with his predecessors in his conception of the drama
as an art form:

Part I: Playwriting

    Chapter 1: Structure
          2: Language (Arias--Lyric)
          3: Music and Rhyming
          4: Dialogue

Part II: Staging

    Chapter 1: Selecting a play
          2: Revising and adapting a play
            Appendices: Two demonstrations

3: Practical guide: music
4: Practical guide: dialogue

Li's dramatic criticism is by no means flawless. At times he contradicts himself, and much too often he is not precise where he could and
should have been. Yet for all his faults, Li Yü was the first Chinese
critic of drama to assign a drama's "poetic language" its proper place
instead of overglorifying it.[27] He is a balanced critic and should be
reckoned with as such.

As an avid theater man, however, Li was understandably preoccupied with the dramatic form popular in his own time. Hence his
criticism applies primarily to ch'uan-ch'i. Only occasionally are Yüan
playwrights mentioned ("Yüan playwrights also read extensively, yet
their plays are free from bookishness," or "Yüan playwrights erred in
this respect [i.e., using vulgar language too often], a shortcoming
stemming from their overreaction against the artificial and elaborate
style . . . "[28] etc.). Even in these brief notices it is not always clear
which group of Yüan dramatists Li was referring to; more often than
not, the context indicates that they may not have been tsa-chü writers
at all. In other words, while Li's Hsien-ch'ing ou-chi is a milestone
in the history of Chinese dramatic criticism, it serves very little to
further our understanding of the Yüan tsa-chü drama; in all probability,
he knew--and cared--less about it than we do.

Thus, for nearly three centuries after the publication of Wang
Chi-te's Ch'ü lü, there was no significant work on Yüan drama. The
modern revival of interest in classical Chinese drama has generally
been ascribed to the efforts of the late Wang Kuo-wei 王國維 (1877-
1927), the scholar to whom all students of Chinese literature will always
remain indebted. The publication of his Hsi-ch'ü k'ao-yüan 戲曲考源
[An Investigation in the Origins of Drama] (1909) and T'ang-Sung ta-ch'ü
k'ao 唐宋大曲考 [Studies in the ta-ch'ü of T'ang and Sung Dynasties]
(1909) caught the immediate attention of scholars of the time.[29] But it
was his Sung-Yüan hsi-ch'ü k'ao 宋元戲曲考 [Studies in Sung and
Yüan Dramas], published in 1912,[30] that laid the foundation for modern
scholarship in the field.[31] Wang Kuo-wei himself claims in his preface
to the book:

> The study of [Chinese drama] was initiated by me, and my
> contribution to it is largely contained in this volume. Not
> that the likes of me are superior to the ancients in talent
> and energy, but the ancients simply never took up the job.[32]

Although we have seen that Wang Kuo-wei is not actually the first in history to pay attention to classical Chinese drama, there is a grain of truth in his gentle arrogance. Wang brought to the field an approach far more scholarly and systematic than his predecessors'. He endeavored to account for the origins of drama (not merely tsa-chü but yüan-pen 院本 and nan-hsi 南戲, as well), tracing them all the way back to ancient times. He pieced together available evidence to reconstruct the milieu of the art form and compiled a bibliography of Yüan plays and biographies of Yüan playwrights. In a chapter on structure, Wang presents us with brief descriptions of the conventions of tsa-chü. In another, on style, he tries to explain the genre's tremendous success in terms of its language.

It is in this latter area that Wang gives himself away: he, too, belongs to the "literary" or "poetic" school which, as we noted, has a long tradition. Sizing up the achievements of Yüan drama, Wang Kuo-wei observes:

> Yüan tsa-chü was a unique universe, and yet the Yüan
> people were not aware of this. . . . For three hundred
> years, most scholars and literati have chosen to neglect
> Yüan dramas and would not see [read] them. [But] those
> who did were all fascinated.[33]

In his considered opinion, "the best part of tsa-chü lies not in its ideas or structure, but in its style, or the wen-chang 文章," and the "mise-en-scène [of tsa-chü] is inferior, needless to say."[34] He sees the success of tsa-chü's style in turn depending heavily on a deft use of language. The use of ch'en-tzu 襯字 or "padding words" and a reliance on colloquialism are chiefly responsible for the straightforwardness and effectiveness that are the hallmarks of the style of Yüan drama. "A new language," Wang declares, "was freely employed in a new genre."[35] These observations are generally quite correct, but the few examples Wang furnishes in support of his thesis (on tsa-chü's excellent style) are all taken from the arias. Given his topic, discussions of prose dialogue are conspicuously lacking. His captious comment that the mise-en-scène of Yüan drama is inferior is particularly unjustified. For the time being, it is important to see Wang's critical stance for what it is--essentially the same as that of his Yüan and Ming peers. Despite his feeble attempt to "raise" Yüan tsa-chü to an equal footing with Greek drama as drama,[36] Wang's enthusiasm for the genre differs from his predecessors only in degree, not in kind.

The major figures in tsa-chü criticism from Yüan times down to the turn of the twentieth century showed appreciation for only the poetic qualities in a dramatic art form. Since long traditions, like old habits, die hard, it is only to be expected that this "poetic fallacy" is still stubbornly with us. The fact is underscored when no less a great contemporary scholar of Yüan drama than Professor Cheng Ch'ien 鄭騫 openly professes his prejudice:

> . . . I have a biased view: I consider the cream, the
> literary merit, of Yüan tsa-chü to lie chiefly in its arias. . . .[37]

By identifying that cream with "literary merit," he has confessed to his neglect of tsa-chü as integrated drama. In all fairness, however, it must also be pointed out that even in his approach to the poetry of the genre Cheng Ch'ien has demonstrated that he is a more rigorous critic than all the others put together. His many contributions[38] to the field have inspired tsa-chü students of this generation.

The "Socialist" Cult

Another notable critical position tends to treat Yüan dramas, particularly those dealing with lawsuits, as manifestations of social protest. It, too, has a long history, dating back to as early as mid-Ming dynasty. The oft quoted--or misquoted--passage is a section on "Yüan ch'ü" 元曲 [Yüan lyrics and/or drama] found in Hu Shih's 胡侍 notebook called Chen-chu ch'uan 真珠船 [The Pearl Boat] (1548).[39] There Hu cites a number of collections of Yüan lyrics and some individual Yüan dramas (which he terms "ch'uan-ch'i," after the fashion of his day) and commends them as being "gently flowing and well-rounded in tone, grand and heroic in spirit" (音調悠圓，氣魄宏壯). The masters of the preceding dynasty had obviously created artifacts with which "the works of later generations simply cannot stand comparison." The reason, he explains, is this:

> For the top ministries in the central government, the chief
> offices in local governments, and posts of any prominence
> were in those days all filled by their own countrymen [i.e.,
> the Mongols]. In most cases, people of the central regions
> [the Chinese] sank to the bottom and served as subordinates,
> unable to realize their ambitions.[40]

To substantiate his observation, Hu goes on to enumerate a few cases of compromised talents, contending that "there were many others who had to settle for clerical jobs and did not acquire the least degree of distinction in their lifetimes." As a result, according to Hu, these people

> applied their useful talent to such trivia as sounds and songs [theater], simply to give vent to their feelings of unhappiness and melancholy: they were truly people who cried out for not getting their fair share.[41]

In other words, drama (and, for that matter, dramatic lyric) flourished in Yüan times precisely because the contemporary men of letters were denied the rosy road to officialdom and, ultimately, political fame, with which their fate had traditionally been associated and interwoven. For this lack of a "nobler pursuit," they had to condescend and turn to the theatrical world.

The view was uncritically shared by another Ming writer, Li K'ai-hsien 李開先 (1501-1568). In his Hsien-chü chi 閑居集 [Collected Works from a Leisurely Life], [42] Li quotes the above words of Hu Shih and further asserts flatly that "this explains the rise of Yüan drama as well as the fall of the Yüan regime."[43] A casual, objective statement of fact was thus elaborated into a critical axiom: "Political discrimination gives birth to new literary genres."

Nevertheless, with what degree of accuracy does this axiom account for the advent of tsa-chü? How much does such a formula, neat as it is, reveal of Yüan drama? And how useful is it as a critical concept? A lot of doubts have to be removed before one can subscribe to such a theory. Indeed, the whole matter of the sudden and "dramatic" blossoming of Yüan tsa-chü is much too complicated to be disposed of in a simple phrase. To be sure, literati of the time played their part, contributing to the furtherance, popularity, and perhaps respectability of tsa-chü both as a literary genre and as a performing art. Their effort is easily recognizable and readily acknowledged. However, to attribute the birth and bloom of tsa-chü on the theatrical and literary scene solely to the discontent of the elite is sheer oversimplification. One needs--if only to do justice to the complexity and importance of the problem--to look into such areas as the relationship between tsa-chü and its precursors (of which there are many), and to consider the economic condition of the late-Sung and Yüan periods as well as the rise of the urban bourgeoisie as an influential social class.[44] In short, the origins of tsa-chü is an issue of great complexity. But since it need not be resolved here, suffice it to say that the formula reached by Li K'ai-hsien is too simplistic to be usable.

Even so, the formula has more recently been pushed further along lines first surveyed by Ming critics. Primarily in the hands of "Marxist" critics in mainland China, the formula has taken on a socialist dimension. Because Yüan playwrights were malcontents, so goes the reasoning, they consequently injected severe social criticism--implicit or explicit--into all they wrote. The result is that there must be much of that inevitable revolutionary trait--the theme of class struggle--in most Yüan dramas.

Hsieh Wan-ying 謝婉瑩, in an article published in 1927,[45] displayed a strong inclination toward such a theory. She divided Yüan plays into two categories according to content and style: the peaceful (because resigned) and the radical (or militant). The targets of the latter were "the darkness of political system of the reign" and "the inequity of wealth in the society"; and these plays "deserve to be called literature of blood and tears."[46] Hsieh even went so far as to suggest that, to Yüan playwrights, "words were vehicles of revolution."[47]

An important figure among later exponents of the socialistic viewpoint is Cheng Chen-to 鄭振鐸. Accounting for the popularity of courtroom plays, he writes:

> The courtroom plays were created, not merely to give the audience a delight in the story, nor merely to provide it with a sensational piece of news: they were in fact serious expositions of the injustice and darkness of the contemporary society.
>   When the common folk watched the courtroom plays, they were seeking not just pleasure from a story, but also some gratification--the vision of justice and lawfulness on the stage! In the darkest era governed by a minority group, they contented themselves the way a man might enjoy a good meal vicariously passing by a butcher shop.[48]

Within the context of the kung-an category, Cheng's observation, though hardly justified, is at least understandable. After all, justice is certainly an unmistakable theme in plays of that division. By being selective and cautious in the application of the theory, Cheng probed the problem in a way becoming his scholarship. Despite his beliefs, however, the sense of injustice is not necessarily part of a sense of class: more likely, in fact, it is highly personal.

If Cheng showed restraint and judiciousness applying the Marxist-socialist formula, his colleagues have taken greater liberties. Chu

Tung-jun 朱東潤 , for example, carefully documented his article on Yüan drama and its times[49] in a professed attempt to evaluate the accomplishment of Yüan playwrights for the social relevance exhibited in their works. He charges that modern readers tend to disregard "the permeating pain and cries [discernable] between the lines in tsa-chü."[50] To him, even the lighter moments in some of the plays, when sparkles of mirth and joviality burst out, are mere illusions. For, he maintains,

> what we see in Yüan tsa-chü are the blood and tears of a
> conquered people. Some of these men suffered so much
> that they became numb and insensitive; from numbness and
> insensitivity came decadence; from decadence came hedon-
> ism. But although epicureans they became, there were,
> in the eyes of mirth, glittering tears of sadness. Besides,
> some of them were [full of] cries under pain--a form of
> deliverance in utter hopelessness.[51]

A majority of the examples Chu furnishes in support of his argument are from plays of the courtroom category, but he seems to believe earnestly that the highly conventional Yüan dramas are in fact literature of protest: a marvelous case of the incompatibility of Marxism and common sense.

The phrase "literature of protest," along with such variants as "people's literature" and "literature of revolution," caught on with many a critic in the fifties and sixties. It is not surprising, then, to find that in a collection of essays devoted to dramatic criticism,[52] all five articles on Kuan Han-ch'ing sound one and the same note--the unbending will of this Yüan playwright to fight out the class struggle and the revolutionary import of his plays. That these critics favor the courtroom plays over the other types is only natural. While all other categories of drama fit their formula even less well, in courtroom plays it is at least easier for them to find what they are determined to find. Talking about the Judge Pao plays, for instance, a Marxian critic has the following to say:

> These Judge Pao plays did not cover up the realities of the
> contemporary society. The powerful and influential in the
> tsa-chü were the feudal lords of the upper stratum, who
> truly enjoyed privilege. The exposé of their sinful deeds
> and the attack on the sordid politics of the time are the
> most valuable achievement of the Judge Pao plays of
> Yüan Dynasty.[53]

But to make generalizations on "the most valuable achievement" of the whole Yüan repertory takes far more research than these critics have undertaken, and certainly far better judgment than they have exhibited.

Granted that these studies, to a certain degree, have their merit, there are a couple of points that need to be made clear at this juncture. First, it is one thing to relate the rise of tsa-chü to the political predic- ament suffered by the literati; it is quite another to read into their works stronger-than-usual sentiments of disenchantment tantamount to advocacy of revolution. While the former approach has been proved to be patently naive from the viewpoint of literary evolution, the latter verges on mis- representation of historical facts. Modern scholarship indicates that the Yüan reign under the Mongols has probably been painted blacker than it actually was, and the hardship people were subjected to was probably less, and more localized, than some of these critics would like to believe.[54] Take, for instance, one of the much-condemned institutions, usury. Time and again, it has been charged that usury, known as yang-kao-li 羊羔利 [the sheep bears a lamb's worth of profit], with an annual interest rate as high as 100 percent, was one of the archevils created by the incompetence of alien rulers, and that it was responsible for many a tragic event depicted so heartrendingly in Yüan drama. The oft cited example is the play Injustice to Tou Ngo: Tou T'ien-chang sells his child Tou Ngo to Granny Ts'ai because he cannot pay back his debt which doubled in the span of one year; the quack doctor attempts on the life of Granny Ts'ai because he cannot pay back his debt; etc. Quod erat demonstrandum: had it not been for the vice of usury, Tou Ngo would not have suffered all the cruelties and injustices that she experiences so excruciatingly in the play.

In fact, however, this kind of usury was not a long-standing evil. It was practiced temporarily at the beginning of the Yüan era--and then in the black market only. To be fair to the Mongol rulers, it should be further pointed out that Emperor Shih-tsu 世祖 (Kublai; r. 1260-1294) even initiated a kind of government loan called wo-t'o ch'ien 斡脱錢 [ortaq money], with an annual interest rate of 18 percent. Although this loan policy was in effect probably only under the reigns of Emperors Shih-tsu and Ch'eng tsung 成宗 (r. 1295-1307), it does show that the image of Mongol rulers as totally and constantly insensitive to the needs of their subjects has probably been exaggerated.[55]

Historical inaccuracy aside, the socialistic school, as criticism, suffers from a much more serious drawback. Ever so avid in their pursuit of sociopolitical content, critics of this school frequently read

into Yüan plays their own political beliefs, quite often seeing what is
not there, and being blind to what is. Such enthusiasm for doctrine
has resulted in not a few studies that scrutinize the "thematic" aspects
of tsa-chü to the exclusion of other important aesthetic ingredients--
especially when the latter do not work in favor of the critic's thesis.
Plays purported to have been meant as relentless attacks on the ruling
class have all been, over the years, well-received by socialist critics--
sometimes regardless of clear deficiency in structure, language, or
character manipulation. For instance, such a mediocre play as Lu
Chai-lang 魯·齋郎 has been proclaimed "one of the very best among the
Yüan dramas."[56] To be sure, thematic study as an approach to literature is as legitimate as it is indispensible. Yet it is hardly the sole
criterion by which such a complex art form as tsa-chü should be judged.
This is especially the case when the very validity of the critic's assump-
tion is called into question. Taken alone, thematic study is no more a
reliable approach to Yüan drama than Yüan drama was a true mirror
of the dark and despotic rule of its time, as some people are wont to
believe.[57] Failing to account for the artistry of tsa-chü, Marxian
critics reveal their own incompetence; their strained and crabbed
doctrinaire interpretation does great injustice to the very dramas they
would approve of.

Some Modern Trends

    The third type of tsa-chü criticism is more or less a modern and
"foreign" phenomenon, for it represents efforts undertaken by predom-
inately Japanese and American scholars since the turn of the century.
Well informed of the findings of modern Chinese scholars (notably Wang
Kuo-wei and, more recently, Cheng Ch'ien), they nevertheless have
come up with some refreshingly new and daring interpretations in which
there is no lack of insight. A marvelous feat that they have performed
is to turn the odds against them to their advantage. Cultural and geo-
graphical separation seem not be crippling factors but enabling ones in
their achievement: there is a healthy "aesthetic distance" between this
group of critics and Yüan drama. Their respect for the poetic language
has not blinded them to the tremendous vitality and interest of tsa-chü
prose dialogue; and their sympathy toward Yüan playwrights has not
tempted them to reduce the dramas to a simplistic Marxist formula.
When most Chinese scholars are plagued by traditions and caught in
the perennial dilemma of either having been trained in the "poetry"
school or having joined the socialist cult (or both), these foreign critics
come closer to seeing tsa-chü as it is: a dramatic form in which

conventions, structure, and manipulation of characters play as important roles as, say, language, singing, or dancing. Indeed, it is with these critics that the dramatic aspects of Yüan tsa-chü begin to receive scholarly attention.

Among Japanese sinologists, Aoki Masaru 青木正兒 is without doubt a towering giant whose greatest contribution has lain in the area of classical Chinese drama. In his Gennin zatsugeki josetsu 元人 雜劇序說 [Introductory Remarks on Yüan Tsa-chü] (1929),[58] Aoki voices his dissatisfaction with the "poetic" critics and offers, as an antidote, critiques on the dramatic construction of the plays he considers "representative" of Yüan tsa-chü. The book looks less awesome today than when it was first published; its discussions of various plays and playwrights often end up being little more than synopses, but the distinction Aoki makes between wen-ts'ai 文采 [elaborate style] and pen-se 本色 [unadorned style] may still serve as a point of departure for serious critical investigation of style in Yüan drama.[59]

Yoshikawa Kōjirō's 吉川幸次郎 Gen zatsugeki kenkyū 元人雜劇 研究 [Studies in Yüan Drama], produced in 1948,[60] is an insightful work, well conceived and well executed. In the first half, on "background," Yoshikawa speculates on the intended audience of tsa-chü and the education of the playwrights--a discussion that sheds considerable light on how Yüan drama may have evolved. But it is the second part that contributes more to our understanding of tsa-chü as dramatic literature. There he concentrates on structure and language. Concerning the former, Yoshikawa persuades us that, in spite of the formal and musical elements working against it, Yüan playwrights somehow managed to give their works a kind of plausibility and verisimilitude. On language, his attention is drawn equally to arias and dialogue; and he goes further than Wang Kuo-wei (on whose works he draws for much of his theorizing) to demonstrate some of their features as they contrast with other genres.

A younger scholar, Iwaki Kudeo 岩城秀夫, has interests even more varied and leans toward the dramas' theatrical aspects. The second part of his Chūgoku gikyoku engeki kenkyū 中國戲曲演劇 研究 [Studies on the Chinese Drama] [61] includes, among other things, articles on the characterization of Judge Pao in the courtroom plays, concepts concerning the structure of tsa-chü, the Ming palace and performances, and the function of Wu 吳 dialect in southern drama.

In the United States, Professor J. I. Crump has contributed more to the field than anyone else. Besides being a felicitous translator,[62] he has in many an article noted the conventions of tsa-chü and speculated on their implications; he has attempted to define the use of language as it relates to the "drama" of the play; and he has expounded some of the more important concepts in tsa-chü criticism.[63] In his forthcoming book, Chinese Theater in the Days of Kublai Khan, he sifts through the vast raw material of extant play scripts and attempts to reconstruct the liveliness of the Yüan theater for us. Among other significant contributions, Dale Johnson's work on prosody[64] (which owes its inspiration to that master of Yüan drama, Cheng Ch'ien) has greatly relieved the burden of later scholars. Georgy Hayden, mentioned above, has established the subgenre of courtroom plays and outlined their structural features. Chung-wen Shih's The Golden Age of Chinese Drama: Yüan Tsa-chü[65] may perhaps be faulted for being too general, yet it treats the genre rightly as drama or at least dramatic literature.

Chinese scholars' efforts in the same direction should not go unnoticed. Since the turn of the century, increased contacts with foreign literatures have stimulated some Chinese critics to take a second look at their own classical drama. The results are varied. Wang Kuo-wei, whom we have noted above, argues that not only are there tragedies among Yüan tsa-chü but the "most tragic" of them, like Injustice to Tou Ngo and The Orphan of Chao (Chao-shih ku-erh 趙氏孤兒), "do not look bad at all even when placed among the greatest of world tragedies."[66] Ch'ien Chung-shu 錢鐘書 on the contrary contends that "whatever value our old [Yüan] drama may have as stage performances or as poetry, they cannot as dramas hold their own with great Western dramas."[67] While Wang shows no convincing evidence to support his claim, Ch'ien errs in imposing on Chinese drama alien standards. It is one thing to say that China has yet to produce great dramas in the Western tradition; it is quite another to conclude that there is no great classical Chinese drama. If Aristotle had laid down any rules for dramatic composition, they would have been concocted in accordance to his concept of drama, as he understood it at the time. To judge Western dramas of other periods (e.g., the Elizabethan) by Aristotelian criteria would be unfair; to judge the classical drama of China by them is as unjust as faulting Western drama because it lacks complex poetic meter, music and modal organization.

In contrast, Professor James J. Y. Liu has demonstrated how knowledge of foreign literatures may be used to illuminate one's own native literature. In his article "Elizabethan and Yüan,"[68] some important conventions of the two theaters are the focus of comparison. Since the comparative method implies seeing things in different lights instead of taking them as islands unto themselves, the method is especially

helpful when the significance or implication of things being compared
has, through long habit, gone undetected or unchallenged. On the other
hand, the brevity of Professor Liu's comparison seems also to alert us
to the futility of a purely "comparative" method by which the classical
Chinese tsa-chü drama would be discussed in the same breath, as it
were, with all Western theater. The observation of the superficial
resemblances or differences in form does not enhance very much our
understanding of the theaters so compared.

Most recently, Chinese scholars in Taiwan have shown renewed
interest in the field. A number of essays under the series title of
"Modern Views on Yüan Tsa-chü" have since December 1975 been published in the Chung-wai Literary Monthly (Chung-wai wen-hsüeh 中外
文學).69 These essays have uniformly treated the tsa-chü as dramatic
literature, a healthy break with the traditional approaches. Some of
them, however, suffer from relying too heavily on Western dramatic
theories (which fit the requirements of an illusionist theater) and ignoring
their incompatibility with tsa-chü convention. It is ironic that these
critics should have just freed themselves from one form of literary
tyranny only to fall victim to another. As long as the fervor for the
genre is kept up, however, there is no doubt that their efforts will bear
fruit and make a significant contribution to the study of Yüan drama.

Approach of the Present Study

With the three major critical approaches thus outlined, no apology
appears necessary if the present writer hopes to break with both poetic
and socialistic traditions and go along with the "dramatic" school. In
general, the attention of this study is focused on the dramas as represented by the surviving texts themselves. In the sense that it entails
close reading of the plays, the method informing this undertaking is, as
has been said, basically one of explication de texte.

Specifically, the investigation is conducted with two premises:
one, that all these Yüan plays are themselves organic wholes; and two,
that each has its own individual character. It is unavoidable that aspects
of drama have to be taken up separately. Emphasis will be placed on
language and the maneuvering of characters, which seem to me the
touchstone for the playwright's craft in such a conventionalized art form
as Yüan tsa-chü. Nevertheless, every effort will be made to see the
merits and defects holistically. That is, each in its relation to the other
elements: the parts are examined and criticized in light of their contribution to the whole.

Since Yüan tsa-chü is a genre abounding in conventions that are strictly adhered to, regularly including stock characters and scenes containing familiar blocks of dialogue with slight variations, it is easy for the reader to lose sight of what individuality each of the plays has. Special attempts will therefore be made in this study to point out how each play of the double-trial group differs from the others. This turns out to be a matter of perceiving how individual playwrights exploit the conventions by supplying their own inventions.

The Texts

Lastly, there is the consideration of usable texts. Tsang Mao-hsün's YCH, mentioned earlier, has long been popular, but since the discovery of the Yüan edition of thirty plays (known as Yüan k'an-pen 元刊本 [Yüan edition]) as well as various Ming texts older than YCH, Tsang's anthology has suffered considerably in stature because of his alleged--and proven--tampering. But although the accusation is justified, the fact still remains that it is on balance the best edition available. The Yüan text, for all its claim as the most authentic (because the earliest), contains literally nothing other than the arias of the leading roles, not to mention its obvious corrupt condition. The admirable and greatly appreciated service Cheng Ch'ien rendered in carefully editing this only extant Yüan text[70] has immensely enhanced its usability; yet there is simply no way to reconstruct the omitted dialogue--an essential part if we do not wish the dramatic side of tsa-chü to continue to be neglected. In its limited way, the Yüan text may serve for the purpose of collation; for dramatic criticism, however, it is an inadequate source to work with if used alone.[71] As to the other Ming texts, the fact that they are different from YCH and similar to each other[72] is no ground on which to conclude that they are necessarily closer to the original; as has been suggested,[73] they might well be from another source, also altered. Unfortunately, it appears that the lack of "authentic" Yüan texts will continue to hamper critics in the field. In the present study, I am an eclectic so far as the texts go. YCH and Yüan ch'ü-hsüan wai-pien 元曲選外編 (WP) [Supplements to YCH][74] serve as the basic texts but, wherever available and feasible, other editions are consulted for elucidation of the plays under consideration.

II. LANGUAGE AS CRITERION
IN YÜAN DRAMA GENERALLY

In the study of Yüan tsa-chü, the use of language constitutes a prime area of exploration--and for good reasons. In the absence of the music for this music-drama, the lyrics written to the arias furnish us with the only clues to the great importance music must have had in the composition, performance, and appreciation of the genre. The complex strictures under which these lyrics were composed, furthermore, provide tsa-chü with its tight formal structure apparent even to a modern reader.

In another direction, language is closely associated with the theatrical aspect of tsa-chü. On a nearly barren stage, it is the only vehicle through which necessary scenery can be constructed for the audience. From time to time, it also conveys stage directions and indicates stage properties.

If we take a close look at it, we find that tsa-chü consists not simply of aria lyrics interspersed with prose, but rather of at least three levels of language, all formally and functionally distinguishable. They are: lyric, represented by arias; prose, constituting most of the dialogue; and verse, most often appearing as an entrance or exit piece, but frequently also used for soliloquy of several types. Each of the three language styles seems to have a particular role to play. It is with this aspect--language levels and their dramatic functions--of the judgment reversal plays of Yüan tsa-chü that the present chapter is concerned.

Lyrical poetry, with its density of meaning and exploitation of figures of speech, is appropriate in expressing intense emotions and subtle feelings. Its elaborateness, in addition, suits the fixed tsa-chü practice of a single singing role in the performance that serves as the vehicle of choice for the "star" of the play. A case in point (though it lies outside our courtroom dramas) is Pai P'u's 白樸 The Rain on the

21

Wu-t'ung Tree (Wu-t'ung yü, YCH, #21 梧桐雨). In this play about the love of a deposed, forlorn emperor for his beloved Kuei-fei (Precious Consort) whom he was forced to decapitate, lyric is used at greater length than in almost any other. For example, halfway through the last act, the dethroned monarch is dreaming of a reunion with his dead beloved when suddenly rain on the wu-t'ung tree disturbs him: [1]

Ex-emperor: (Sings) [to the tune of]

雙鴛鴦 Shuang yüan-yang

Her phoenix-winged hat with its emerald green lies
    aslant
Just as she was wont to come from her bath,
Reflecting so seductively in the cloud screen.[2]
Startled from this lovely half-done reverie,
    I find
Half my silk lapel drenched with tears of love.

蠻姑兒 Man ku-erh

Vexed and perturbed am I.
But what wakened me was not geese passing by the
    tower,
Nor the winter cricket chirping by the wall,
Nor the jade horse wind-chime tinkling under the eave,
Nor the bronzy rooster standing on his perch.
It was the rushing rain on the wu-t'ung tree
    outside the window.
Sound on sound it spatters sere leaves;
Drop by drop it drips on chilly twigs;
Torturing my grieving soul.

滾繡球 Kun hsiu-ch'iu

Oh this rain! No drought-parched sprouts to save,
Nor dried grass to moisten,
Nor flowers to set abloom.
Who would look forward to the balm of autumn rain
When the twigs are blue
And the branches green as jade?
Now the tapping a thousand times that of the
    rain on the plantain leaves,
It keeps dropping, dropping, like a thousand pearls.
And urns and basins are overbrimming with water.
Raining the whole night through, it drives one mad.

叨叨令　<u>Tao-tao ling</u>

First the rain falls swiftly, like a myriad pearls
　　　dropping on a jade plate;
Then resounding like bands playing before a royal
　　　banquet.
Now the sound is clear like a spring-fed waterfall
　　　gushing from a green, rocky mountain top;
Now urgent like battle drums under embroidered
　　　banners.
How it vexes me,
Oh, how it vexes me,
This noisy changing sound of rain!

倘秀才　<u>T'ang hsiu-ts'ai</u>

Spate after spate beats the fading leaves of the
　　　<u>wu-t'ung</u> tree;
Drop by drop it drips until my heart is broken.
Why is this tree tightly guarded by the silver
　　　railings of the golden well?
Better to have down every last twig for fuel and
　　　kindling!
<u>(Interrupting himself, says)</u>
It was under this tree when Kuei-fei first danced
the Green Plate Dance; it was also by this tree when
we exchanged our secret vows. Now when I was
seeking her in my dream, it was again this tree
that wakened me.
(Sings)　　滾繡球　Kun Hsiu-ch'iu

That night in the Palace of Longevity
We pledged our love while walking along the
　　　winding corridor.
We shouldn't have leaned, shoulder to shoulder,
　　　against the <u>wu-t'ung</u> tree--
Our words were constantly interrupted by its
　　　noisy whispers.
That morning in the Pavillion of Deep Fragrance,
While Dancing <u>Ni-shang</u> and <u>Liu-yao</u>,
I beat the rhythm with my red ivory chopsticks.
The rustling of that tree blurred the music.
Looking back,
The mirthful meetings of times gone by
Must have sown the seeds of the cheerless present.

Eunuch (<u>says</u>): My lord, all other plants make noise
 when the rain falls on them, not just the <u>wu-t'ung</u>.
Ex-emperor (<u>says</u>): Ah, how little you know! Let me
 tell you:

(He sings)   三 煞   San-sha

The willow rain is moist and misty,
Chilling the house as it
Invades the curtains and the screens.
The plum rain, as fine as strands of silk,
Decorates with silver drops the whole pavillion by
   the riverside.
The apricot blossom rain wets and reddens the
   balustrade.
The pear blossom rain presents a look fair yet
   lonesome.
The lotus blossom rain urges the floating blue
   leaves to dance.
The bean blossom rain makes the green leaves
   look desolate.
But none of these resembles you, oh rain, which
   shakes my soul and shatters my dream;
Increasing my regret, adding to my sorrow,
The whole night through.
No doubt the water fairy is out amusing herself
With a willow branch spattering water to the winds.

二 煞   Erh-sha

Spattering, like propitious whales by the banks
   of the pond,
Scratching, like spring silkworms nibbling at
   the leaves over mulberry frames.
Spilling down the jade-steps, it is a clepsydra;
Down through the carved eavespouts, it drops
   like wine dripping to the new vat.
It will keep raining till the watches wear away
   and the clepsydra stops, when
The candle is out and its fragrance gone.
I know now how Kao Feng, that summer, allowed
   the rain to wash his wheat away.

黃鐘煞 Huang-chung sha

Riding the west wind, the rain whistles low through
    the screened windows;
Bringing a chilly draft, it frequently knocks at the
    boudoir.
I wonder if heaven has not purposely roused my
    sorrowful melancholy.
Like the bells of passage sounding sadly along the
    Trestled Road,
Like Hua-nu's lay with a barbarian drum,
Like Po-ya playing the Water Fairy's melody,
The rain washes the chrysanthemums, soaks the
    fence,
Drowns the little island and scours the stone cracks,
Saturates the dying lotus and overflows the pond,
Moistens the last butterflies wearing off the powder
    from their wings,
Drenches the flying lightning bugs till their
    lights no longer glow.
At the green window the crickets are chirping;
The sound of wild geese high above approahces.
The anvils of dawn sound everywhere,
Bringing a new chill to the unaccustomed hour.
Now I realize the night's rain has kept me on edge,
Accompanied by the drip-drop of the water clock.
The rain increases,
My tears are no fewer.
Rain has wetted the chilled twigs,
As my tears have soaked my dragon robe;
Neither would cease:
Separated by the wu-t'ung tree,
Both have kept falling till dawn.

(YCH, pp. 362-64)

    Taken out of context, as it is here, the lover's complaint may
appear almost trifling and capricious, his argument labored and arbitrary, his conceits far-fetched and irrelevant. But Pai P'u is concerned with the effect of Kuei-fei's death on her lover who, though an
emperor, had to order her execution under constraint. Neither history
nor monarchy matters here; what is at stake is the drama within the
protagonist. The intense emotion of that inner drama is presented
obliquely but movingly in the highly charged lyricism just quoted.

The rain on the wu-t'ung tree brings out a fantastic number of tiny observations and images that give immediacy and realism and even urgency to the lover's grieving. They fall into two groups, contrasting and complementing each other. On one hand, there are bright, color- ful ones, symbolic of the glorious palace life and of the past when the Precious Consort was still alive, warm, and vital. I refer to the "phoenix-winged hat," "cloud screen," "blue" twigs, "branches green as jade," "a myriad pearls dropping on a jade plate," "bands playing before a royal banquet," "embroidered banners," "silver railings of the golden well," "screened windows," "boudoir," "dragon robe," and so on.

Juxtaposed to these are images with a sense of decay, of fading away, symbolic of the dethroned old man's present state of mind. Included in the latter group are "sere leaves," "chilly twigs," "drought- parched sprouts," "dried grass," "fading leaves," "the watches wear away [literally, 'waning, closing']," "clepsydra stops [literally, 'broken, severed']," "have down every last twig," "dying lotus," "last butterflies," etc. The distinction between these two sets of images is sometimes blurred ("silk lapel drenched with tears of love," for instance)--just as the protagonist's feelings and memories are mixed, of course.

There are other images (such as those of the heavenly, the immor- tal) and poetic devices (such as onomatopoeia), all used with great effectiveness. But the juxtaposition of the images described above amply manifests the "conflict," as it were, of the quondam monarch. Perceived in this light, the fourth act is rightly the "climax" of Rain on the Wu-t'ung Tree, in which the impact of Kuei-fei's death--not her death per se--is the focus of attention. One can therefore sympathize with the ex-emperor who suspects that, like flies to wanton boys, he has been the sport of the gods:

> No doubt the water fairy is out amusing herself
> With a willow branch spattering water to the winds.

Or, more explicitly:

> I wonder if heaven has not purposely roused my
> sorrowful melancholy.

The fickleness of fate, the transitory nature of love and joy, and the helplessness of man before them both--these, it seems to me, are the central themes of Rain; and, through seemingly capricious and oblique lyrics which have been criticized as being "just too long,"[3] they come forth, powerful and overwhelming.

Lyrics, with their dignity of diction, vivid metaphors, and rich connotations, are effective means of conveying subtle yet powerful emotions and feelings. They are not conducive to narration, however; where lyrics flourish, the forward movement of the story line tarries, which is not necessarily a bad thing. The dramatist in Rain (cited above), for instance, dwells by choice on the emotional reaction of the bereaved former emperor, taking time and pains to give the most minute and intimate portrait of an ardent love dying in the ashes of loneliness. But there are places in every drama where the plot has to be carried onward, if only to meet minimum requirements of the play and set the scene for further arias; this, of course, is the major province of prose.

For our purpose, let me use Ma Chih-yüan's 馬致遠 Autumn in the Palace of Han (Han-kung ch'iu, 漢宮秋 YCH, #1), the third act of which demonstrates how the balanced use of arias and prose arouses the deepest emotion and at the same time preserves the outline of the "story." Like Rain, Autumn depicts the helplessness of man, however great his worldly power may be, in avoiding the bitterest of human sorrows. The sorrow is parting at death (死別 szu-pieh) in the former play; in the latter, it is separation during life (生離 sheng-li)--and for life!

The emperor of Han is forced to part with Chao-chün, his newly met favorite consort, who is to be sent away to the Tartar Khan to keep peace in the realm. When the emperor finds himself obliged to choose against his will, he realizes his own inadequacy: for all his power as the head of an empire, he has to submit to the whims of a "barbarian" chief. It is this sense of inadequacy that brings out the most eloquent passage of the play when ravaged autumn scenery reminds the emperor of the autumn in himself--not the autumn of harvest but that of desolation, brought on by the victorious advance of winter's legions. He sings:

梅花酒 Mei-hua chiu

Before me lie the bleak and ravaged plains,
The grass has yellowed, stricken by the frost,
The mottled coats of dogs grow gray and shaggy.
. . . .
She, yes, she brokenhearted said good-bye;
I, yes, I took her hand and climbed the bridge.

She and her train ride into the desert;
I in my carriage return now to the palace.
I pass the wall and follow a twisting lane,
A twisting lane that leads close to her room,
Close to her room where the moon grows dusky;
The moon grows dusky and the night turns cold,
The night turns cold and the [crickets] weep.
The [crickets] weep by green-curtained windows,
By green-curtained windows that feel nothing.
To feel nothing! Only a man of steel
Could feel nothing. No! Even a man of steel
[Beset by such] grief would shed a thousand
      trickling tears. . . .

(<u>YCH</u>, p. 10)[4]

For the ministers of the court, the betrothal of Chao-chün is a successful and clever diplomatic move that forestalls an impending national
crisis. For the emperor, however, it marks the beginning of a personal misery that can only be cured by time--if indeed it can be cured
at all. Without Chao-chün, nothing can be the same. The anguish and
anxiety of the emperor is poured out in the vein of emotional logic.

As in <u>Rain</u>, there is a large quantity of lyrical poetry in this play;
but here prose is used for other purposes than merely serving as pauses
or providing new arena for poetic exploitation--which is exactly what the
eunuch's scanty interjections do in the last act of <u>Rain</u> (see p. 24, above).
In <u>Autumn</u>, shortly after the aria quoted above, the scene is shifted to
another part of the border, where the following dialogue takes place:

Chao-chün: Where are we now?

Envoy: This is the Amur River, the boundary between our
    territories and those of the Han. The lands to the south
    belong to the Han, and those to the north to us.

Chao-chün: Will your highness give me a cup of wine that I
    may pour a libation facing the south, and take a last leave
    of China before my long journey? (She pours a libation.)
    Mighty emperor of the Han! Now is this life ended. I
    await you in the next. (She throws herself into the river.)

(The Khan, alarmed, tries to save her, but fails.)

Khan (in tears): Alas, alas. Chao-chün was so unwilling
to enter my domains that she threw herself into the
river and died. Let her be buried, then, on the bank
of this river at a place we shall call the Green Mound.
She whom I thought to marry is dead. In vain did I
create enmity between myself and the Han. It was all
schemed by that knave, Mao Yen-shou. Men! Bring
Mao Yen-shou here, then dispatch him under guard to
the Han court, where he will meet his punishment. I
shall resume our traditional alliance with the Emperor
of Han, and remain forever to him as nephew to uncle.
All may have proved for the best. . . .

(YCH, pp. 10-11)[5]

Since here, again as in Rain, the inner drama of the emperor is the
focus, the outward actions become secondary and are treated accord-
ingly. Even the potentially dramatic incident of Chao-chün's suicide
is underplayed; nothing comes of it (at least in the text as we have it
today) except a speech from the Khan in which there is more of politics
than passion. Compare these passages of prose with the preceding
lyrics, and the function of prose to keep up the pace of the play, to
manage "narrative time,"[6] is apparent. The external movement having
been thus resolved, the next and final act may then be--and actually
is--devoted again to the inner drama of the Han emperor until the play
ends when news of Chao-chün's death arrives at the Han court.

Speeding up the plot, however, is not the only function of prose,
which is also closely associated with comic scenes. To be sure, much
of the comic effect of a tsa-chü play (and there is no lack of it in the
judgment reversal group!) is achieved through the liberal use of slapstick; but verbal jokes are a reliable source of fun both more refined
and sophisticated. The fact that these jokes are in prose or doggerel
rhymes to be spoken or recited may be attributed to two reasons. First,
they were meant to be heard as distinctly as possible so that none among
the audience could have missed them. Second, the comic relief thus
achieved--relief both from intense emotions and from strained ears--
might help the audience to a better appreciation of the play when its
arias resume. These theatrical considerations aside, however, the
merit of the humorous elements should be judged by its contribution to
the drama itself. That is, jokes that are in some way integrated with
the development of the theme or characterization should be preferred
over those that are there simply as fillers. And even among the

"relevant jokes," further distinction should be made about the art with which they are introduced or handled. More on this topic when we deal with their representatives in the judgment reversal plays.

Spoken verse, be it in shih 詩 or tz'u 詞 form,[7] occupies a peculiar plane between lyric and prose. For although stylized and more arresting in form than plain prose, it usually falls far short of the elegance and sensuous charm of the aria (which for one thing was always graced by the accompaniment of music). This unique quasi-formal quality of verse makes it a useful tool for certain dramatic purposes. With rhyming, parallelisms, and often poetic diction, verse makes a suitable or even ideal vehicle for minor characters--to whom, it should be remembered, convention has denied the elevated aria--to voice their deeper feelings and higher sentiments. In this way, it helps remedy or modify whatever inconvenience the convention of a single singing role causes.[8] On the other hand, it may also be a valuable source of comic relief. The air of pomp and dignity attendant upon various poetic forms turns the verse into a facile means to mock, to burlesque--when it is assigned to an insignificant character, for example, or applied to trivial subject matter or a farcical situation or all three. The incongruity between form and content seldom fails to trigger comedy of a higher order.

In addition to their flexibility, we should remember that these verses are declaimed or recited, and may therefore be expected to command the audience's full comprehension and draw its immediate response.[9] The playwright can thus depend upon entrance verse, for instance, to give his audience some hint of the personality or intention of a particular character. Or he can reinforce the impression of resoluteness of another by assigning him an exit verse containing such emotions. Or he can resort to a lengthy, controlled piece to underscore the grave or light-hearted nature of a specific situation. The possibilities are many and the dramatic implications tremendous.

To see the verse in operation in Yüan drama as a whole, let us turn to The Orphan of Chao (Chao-shih ku-erh 趙氏孤兒 ; YCH 85)[10] for a moment. A play of revenge, it depicts the Orphan of Chao surviving a merciless massacre that wipes out his entire clan and succeeding, in the end, in avenging his slaughtered kinsmen. The play opens with an entrance verse by T'u-an Ku, Great General of the Kingdom of Tsin:

> Man may not intend to harm the tiger,
> The tiger is determined to wound man!

> If you don't finish your job the first time around,
> You're bound to regret later--in vain!

> (YCH, p. 1476)

From the doggerel that also incorporates a proverb, it would appear
that T'u-an is comparing himself to an innocent man who has to be on
the guard to protect himself from malicious elements. But when he
goes on to recall--not without complacency--his many attempts on the
life of Chao Tun, his political archrival, the audience perceives the
irony of the entrance verse: it is the Great General who has behaved
like the tiger he alludes to. This insight immediately adds a new dimension to the audience's understanding of T'u-an, and its response to what
follows on stage is bound to be modified by such awareness.

Now, T'u-an has already gotten satisfaction from the death of
Chao Tun and his entire clan--except, that is, his son Chao Shuo, whose
tie with the royal family (he is married to the princess) has made T'u-
an's task a bit thorny. Still, it is not beyond the Great General's
craft. Toward the end of his monologue, T'u-an reveals yet another of
his dark plots to "uproot the weed" completely:

> I have sent a messenger with a forged royal edict com-
> manding Chao Shuo to end his own life by one of the
> three formal ways: by a bowstring, a dagger, or
> poisoned wine. . . .

> (YCH, p. 1476)

With this uninhibited avowal T'u-an leaves the stage--but not before he
recites the following piece:

> His three hundred kinsmen already dead,
> Chao Shuo alone survives--he has special ties.
> I'll have uprooted all the weed,
> No matter by which means he dies.

> (YCH, p. 1476)

The exit verse plants firmly in the audience's mind T'u-an's implacable
resolve to wipe out the Chaos entirely. In this sense, it reaffirms the
axiom stated in his entrance piece: "If you don't finish your job the
first time around,/You're bound to regret later--in vain!" Moreover,

the recurrence of the image of uprooting the weed is significant. As we shall see, it is not only a fixation with the Great General; the princess also refers to her child as a "root" (which of course is not an uncommon metaphor). Such being the case, the exit verse puts into sharper focus the interest of the play: Will T'u-an succeed in his attempt to eradicate each and every member of the Chao family?

As it turns out, Chao Shuo does just as T'u-an bids, ending his life with a dagger. But the princess gives birth to a male child and calls this posthumous son by a name with profound implications: the Orphan of Chao. When T'u-an learns of this, he is apprehensive but appears composed and confident as before, with his plan already firmly in mind:

> T'u-an (says): Indeed! Calls him the Orphan of Chao?
> Well, it will be soon enough to kill the child after a
> full month is passed. Have someone bear my com-
> mand to Lieutenant General Han Chüeh and tell him
> to keep guard at the gate of the [princess'] mansion.
> Never mind what goes in, but search all that comes
> out. Anyone found smuggling out the Orphan of Chao
> will have his whole family put to the sword--not one
> of his relatives shall be spared! . . .

(He recites.)

> Little did I expect the princess in a family way.
> The orphan she bore is my deadly enemy.
> After a full month it will be put to sword,
> And only then "I've uprooted them!" will I say.

(Exit.)

(YCH, p. 1478)

The prose portion endows T'u-an with a bold facade, undaunted by the unexpected turn of events. The exit verse, however, betrays his per-turbation and annoyance. It also portrays a resolved Great General, although his characterization of the new-born baby as his "deadly enemy" hardly sheds favorable light on the villain's dwindling stature.

The audience is now set to wonder what clever scheme the princess can possibly come up with in the "grace period" to preserve the child. Her entrance piece offers a clue to the troubled mind of some-one who has every right to complain that the world is too much with her:

> The worries of all mankind
> Weigh heavy on my mind.
> Like the rain of an autumn eve:
> Each drop a cause to grieve.

(YCH, p. 1478)

But, as the audience knew, or confidently expected, there is hope.

The hope of the princess rests with a certain retainer named Ch'eng Ying. She calls him in and goes straight to the heart of the matter: "Somehow smuggle this child out of here and hide him; when he comes of age, let him avenge the Chaos." Fully aware of the tight security and grave consequences that attend this mission, however, Ch'eng does some backing and filling. The princess is desperate, and out of this desperation develops a scene both admirable and touching-- greatly aided by the use of verse:

Princess: Ch'eng Ying,

(She recites.)

> As they say,
> When in peril one thinks of close relatives,
> When in adversity one thinks of old friends.
> If you would safely carry out this dear child of mine,
> The Chaos will have preserved their root.

(She kneels and says.)

> Ch'eng Ying, have pity on the three hundred
> souls of the Chao family: their revenge depends
> on this child!

Ch'eng: Please get up, your Highness. Suppose I succeed in smuggling out your son. When T'u-an gets wind of it, he will demand the Orphan of Chao. And you will tell him that you gave it to me. My whole family would have to die--so be it; but I could not preserve the child either.

Princess: So be it, Ch'eng Ying, I'll let you leave this house with your mind at peace.

(She recites.)

> Have no fear, Ch'eng Ying, in your mind,
> And let me finish--with a thousand streaks of tears.

His father killed himself with a dagger,--

(She takes out an apron-sash to hang herself.)

So be it!
His mother follows closely! (Exit.)

Ch'eng: Little did I think the princess would hang herself!
I dare not stay long. Let me open my medicine chest
and put the child in it. I'll cover his body with some
herbs. Heaven, have mercy! Three hundred and more
of the Chao family have already been wiped out com-
pletely--all except this little child. If I can save him--
well, you'd be lucky, little one, and I'd consider myself successful. If you're discovered, well--you die,
and so does my whole family!

(He recites.)

Here stands Ch'eng Ying searching his thoughts:
The Chao family is pitiful indeed.
If we escape the nine rings of this fortress town
We will have cheated the Nets of Heaven and the
Snares of Earth. (Exit.)

(YCH, pp. 1478-79)

Notice when the princess recites her first verse in the passage
quoted, desperately needing assistance from her husband's retainer,
she resorts to half-veiled speech. The first two lines allude obliquely
to obligations of kinsmen and friends, and it is as a kinsman and friend
that Ch'eng has been received by the Chaos. For, earlier on, Ch'eng
professed that he has been "treated with greater favor than has been
accorded any others," and that fortunately his name "was not on the
family roster" (YCH, p. 1478)--with the implication that it might well
have been. This fact leaves Ch'eng with little choice: he has to shoulder
the responsibility. Notice, too, that the word "root" once again sur-
faces. It drives home the importance of the child, and hence of the mission at hand; but it signals more than that to the audience, pointing to
the lurking threat and brutality of the Great General, to whom extirpa-
tion of this "root" of the Chaos has become a mania.

The princess' next verse is no less significant. It starts by
reminding Ch'eng of his former master's death and ends by directly
involving him in the death of his mistress. Since it is Ch'eng's sense
of insecurity that touched off her suicide, he must bear the albatross

now; he is morally bound to the Chaos. The princess dies in the hope that Ch'eng may leave her house--with the orphan, presumably--with his fears laid to rest; and now Ch'eng cannot leave without the child and still have peace of mind. After this passage, Ch'eng's course is predictable. As his exit poem suggests, hope is still alive for the orphan, although it is admittedly a faint one at this stage.

The above examples from The Orphan of Chao demonstrate that the distinction between verse and prose or lyric in tsa-chü is not just formal; it is functional as well. In an economical and captivating manner (which stems from its form), the verse adds extra dimensions to characters and events. It is that necessary ingredient which makes a dish of Yüan drama taste just right.

*　　*　　*　　*　　*

As a group, the courtroom plays exemplify a balanced use of all three levels of language--in contrast to the predominance of lyric in Autumn and Rain, for example. This phenomenon generally holds true with the plays of judgment reversal. There is heavier reliance on prose because in these plot-oriented dramas forward movement is essential. There are also considerably more occasions for verse as a result of larger casts of dramatis personae and more complicated dramatic situations. The emergence of prose and verse, ideally, should not undercut the importance of lyric; as has been partially demonstrated, each has its own way of contributing to the drama.

Of the seven plays under investigation, The Mo-ho-lo Doll and Injustice to Tou Ngo excel in the use of language. Powerfully moving and highly suggestive, the arias in these two plays do not exist merely as good poetry; they also bear significantly on the drama's setting, plot, and/or theme. The verse and prose portions in both are equally instrumental, if less obtrusive. Rescue of a Filial Son, The Chalk Circle, and The Gold Phoenix Hairpins come second in rank, each boasting brilliant strokes here and there. For instance, the flights of erudition displayed in the arias of Hairpins well become the protagonist who is a scholar; at the same time, their unmistakable bookishness pokes fun at his impracticality. In Rescue, the arias adequately portray a mother both at her most dangerously self-righteous state and at her most humble and tender moments. Some of the recapitulations in verse and prose also enhance our understanding of the characters or the development of the play. Circle abounds in broad jokes in verse and prose, which not only enliven an otherwise gloomy story, but are key to the play's central theme. Comparatively disappointing are Judgment on the Kerchief and The Child Shen-nu-erh, with often unwarranted repetitions and word-play that do not sparkle. (For the scenario of each play, see Appendix, pp. 151-59.)

The Best of the Class

The Mo-ho-lo Doll

Li Te-ch'ang, a merchant, has been away from his hometown to avoid a predicted disaster. Returning, he is detained by a violent rainstorm just outside of the town. Down with a severe chill and fever, he takes shelter in a temple and sends for his wife, Liu Yü-niang. Before she arrives, however, his cousin Li Wen-tao (who covets his wife) has come and poisoned him; so by the time Te-ch'ang gets home, he is already a dead man. Liu Yü-niang, who flatly rejects the proposed settlement of Li Wen-tao, is charged by the latter with keeping a lover and murdering her husband. She is sentenced to death in the first trial, but the second judge, with the assistance of Kao Shan, the doll-peddler who had served as messenger for Li Te-ch'ang, uncovers the truth and reverses the verdict.

Early in the first act, as part of his monologue, Li Te-ch'ang describes the rainstorm as follows:

(Sings)　　　　　點絳唇　Tien chiang-ch'un

The Seventh Month is scarce begun
And Earliest Autumn carries still
The heat of summer days.
But wearing
Light clothes of summer's weight
Can ill protect me from these swooping strands of rain.

混江龍　Hun-chiang lung

Cloud joins cloud relentlessly
The countryside grows indistinct, as seen through
　　　wavering depths of water.
I watched the rain conceal the peaks
And clouds lock up the open blue.

(speaks)

This is a heavy storm!

(sings)

Its cloudy heights as deep as the Eastern Sea,
The press of its rains as heavy as Tung-t'ing Lake,
And
Haze and scud deceive my eye
And hide the road I took.
Black blinding
Clouds on every hand
Dim shimmering
Mists across my path.

(speaks)

Now it's raining even harder!

油葫蘆  Yu hu-lu

(sings)

It is as though
I had become painted into an ink-and-water sketch
    of the Hsiao-Hsiang
Where I am
Soaked through and through.
But all is made worse
By these funneling, tunneling rills scoring their
    runnels.
See their rash spattering dash along the wave-
    havering road.
Hear the wind's
Lush-susurrous brush through the mist-glistening
    trees.
How can I pass by you,
    Loose oozey pool of
    Grime slimy mud
Unless I
    Step trippingly tiptoe
    Shuffle softly and slow?
For I must
Teeter myself upright to totter on ahead. . . .

(YCH, pp. 1369-70)[11]

In conjunction with his translation, Professor Crump points out that here is "a subject that takes particularly well to Chinese lyricism."[12]

The "sound-soaked" English in his rendering has certainly done justice
to the echoics and onomatopoeia in the Chinese. The elaborate poetry
also has dramatic functions to perform. In terms of plot development,
it is this rain that brings the subsequent illness of Li Te-ch'ang, his
message, and ultimately his being foully murdered by his cousin. Thematically, the violent storm suggests a supernatural force at work, and
it is deftly suggested that it is a soothsayer's prophesy--itself a supernatural power--come true. Furthermore, this storm begins to establish
an atmosphere lonely, desolate, and befitting the helplessness of a man
caught in the machinery of fate.

The next moment Li says:

> Way off there is an old temple I can use to get out
> of the rain. (Pantomimes putting down carrying
> pole and hampers.) Now I've put down my load I
> see it is a temple to the Lord Commander of the
> Five Ways and long gone to ruin. . . . what a lonely
> place!

(YCH, p. 1370)[13]

The atmosphere is further established in the aria that follows:

(sings)   醉中天 Tsui-chung t'ien

The sagging altar table does crowd the door ajar,
Wild grass invades the boundaries of the temple
        porch. . . .

(YCH, p. 1370)[14]

The picture is one of a lonely wayfarer cowering in a ruined and deserted
temple because of a ruthless rainstorm--an image that generates a
sense of utter helplessness, the very essence of Li Te-ch'ang's situation.
Consequently, his bootless prayer for the god's protection (YCH, p. 1370)
rings with ironic overtones, particularly when that very god is supposed
to direct souls on their proper roads in the underworld.

Not only in lyric, but in verse and prose as well, the playwright
demonstrates admirable craft. Halfway through the second act, after
he commits the murder, Li Wen-tao, Te-ch'ang's cousin and murderer,
tries to heap blame for the foul deed on the head of his "sister-in-law,"
who refuses to be bullied. When the suit is brought to the court, the

comic Prefect-Judge enters, reciting in doggerel:

> When I'm the judge I hear each plea
> With fine impartiality.
> I take my gold with an open mind
> From defense and plaintiff equally.
> The senior judge would (if he knew)
> Flog me till the cocks all crew.

> (YCH, p. 1375)[15]

In the same vein, when the plaintiff is ordered to kneel down as is customary, the Prefect falls on his knees; the rationale, as he puts it, is that "whoever comes to the court and makes complaint is my daily bread for which I have great respect." The audience was doubtless ready for (indeed, confidently expecting) his horseplay as a counterpoise for the dense gloom of the first act. Exactly what this comment implies is made clear when, toward the end of the act, he splits the bribe with his cunning clerk.

As in so many other courtroom plays, the clerk is simply indispensible because the obtuse prefect is predictably at a loss when it comes to judging. Clerk Hsiao is summoned, who also has an entrance piece:

> The judge is clean as water,
> His clerk, white as flour;
> When the two are mixed together,
> You're in for a muddled picture.

> (YCH, p. 1376)

It does not take the audience long to realize what a truthful account that is, for the following is what happens when Clerk Hsiao, taking charge, sees the plaintiff:

Hsiao: This fellow--he looks familiar. Oh yes, it's the physician. Yesterday, in front of his house, he wouldn't give me so much as a seat, and now he's come to me. Steward, take him away and flog him.

(Steward takes Li away.)

Li (<u>sticking out three fingers</u>): Sir, I'll give you this much.

Hsiao: What's wrong with those other two fingers of yours--
rotted?

(<u>YCH</u>, p. 1376)

Granted, both the stupid judge and the shrewd clerk represent corrupt officialdom (which Yüan drama loves to make the butt of its satire) and are stock characters, particularly in the courtroom plays;[16] they can nonetheless, when handled properly, as here, be integrated with the play and contribute to the significance of the drama. (After all, collages are typically created out of pre-formed parts, but some collages have artistic merit and some have none.) In the case just cited, the comic atmosphere of the courthouse forms a striking contrast to the preceding scenes of gloom and cold-blooded murder. It may be presumed that, having watched Li Wen-tao poison his brother and bully his sister, the audience must have been at the tensest point of their emotion. It may also be presumed that, having listened to twelve arias consecutively, the audience is now ready for a break. So far as audience response is concerned, then, the comic scene presented in verse and prose offers a much-desired relief that probably arrives at a moment shrewdly calculated by the playwright who knew this audience was here to be entertained and diverted, not to be read a doomsday tract.

There is, however, more to the comic scene than these apparent theatrical concerns. The portrayal of the corrupt officials is designed to make the audience feel pessimistic about the prospect of Liu Yü-niang, the defendant, ever getting a fair chance in the trial--a concern that later proves to be justified. On the other hand, perhaps the audience enjoys a <u>frisson</u> of gloom as a contrast to the "happy ending" they confidently expect. Moreover, against the backdrop of the first trial scene, which exhibits preposterousness at its height, the second trial can then gain solemnity and dignity. Compared with their unfeeling, incompetent, and greedy counterparts, the new prefect and <u>his</u> clerk appear admirably concerned with justice. Nevertheless, as is pointed out below (p. 107), the second prefect often depends as much on coercion as the first.

The excellence of language in <u>Doll</u> extends to its various verse declamations. Unlike entrance or exit verses, which are normally couplets or quatrains, declamations are lengthier speeches that generally recapitulate the story and/or point to new directions in the development of the play. In <u>Doll</u>, Liu Yü-niang the defendant, Wang the new prefect, Chang the clerk, and Kao Shan the peddler-messenger all give important declamations; for our purpose, the one Liu Yü-niang recites, in Act III, will suffice:

> I pray, good clerk, indulge me for a time
> While I set forth the sequence of the crime:
> Te-ch'ang, who left to flee malignant fate,
> Brought back a purse ten times its former weight.
> But in a temple sheltering the day
> A morbid illness seized him where he lay.
> He hemorrhaged then and all his portals bled.
> We'd barely reached our gate when he was dead.
> He died from poison; so much I knew.
> I called his brother, asking what to do,
> But he straightway accused <u>me</u> of the crime
> And claimed I kept a lover all the time
> Te-ch'ang was south. Before I could protest
> He hailed me into court. You know the rest.
> They flogged me till I made a false confession--
>   (I'm only a woman!)
> I could not stand their cruel inquisition.
>
> But sir, from childhood I was always Te-ch'ang's wife.
> How could I bring myself to take his life?
> His brother acts from some malign intent--
> Please help, good clerk, for I'm innocent!
>
> (<u>YCH</u>, p. 1378)[17]

Although its content is all new to Clerk Chang to whom it is addressed, the declamation is essentially a recounting of what the audience has already learned firsthand, so to speak. Furthermore, a prose version of approximately the same facts was presented by the defendant to Clerk Hsiao a while ago in the previous trial (<u>YCH</u>, p. 1376). Why, then, the repetition?

The question must be answered on two different levels: the virtues of verse declamation in general and the appropriateness of Liu Yü-niang's speech in particular. As has been pointed out earlier, dramatic verse, being different from the accustomed speech pattern, produces an effect of distinction, while at the same time promoting clarity by the very fact that it is recited rather than sung.[18] Verse achieves orderliness, refinement, precision, and dignity. This leads us to the second

consideration: the particular place of Liu Yü-niang's declamation in
this play. The prose version of the facts was fitted to the farcical context of the first trial. The verse recapitulation is, on the other hand,
connected with the advent of justice, with all that the term implies--
not the least of which is clarity and dignity. Liu Yü-niang's verse, far
from being just another unwarranted repetition, has dramatic significance for the play. We must assume that the playwright did not go to
the trouble of versifying if he did not feel it worth the effort in some way.
(It may be added here that in judgment reversal plays, if there is verse
testimony at all it is given to the honest review judge; the corrupt
official presiding over the first trial invariably gets a prose version.)

Injustice to Tou Ngo

Kuan Han-ch'ing's mastery of language in Injustice to Tou Ngo is
also remarkable, especially with respect to lyric and verse. The play
tells of the sufferings of Tou Ngo, a young widow whose "tragic flaw"
seems to be her unfaltering devotion to moral principle. Because she
would rather die than submit to the lustful Donkey Chang--a good-for-
nothing bully who by chance saved the life of Tou's mother-in-law and
who now seeks Tou's hand in marriage--Chang charges her with poisoning
his father. The case is brought to court, where Tou Ngo withstands the
harshest of tortures only to be defeated, in the end, by her own filial
piety: rather than see her aged mother tortured as she herself has been,
Tou chooses to confess to the false charge that costs her life. (See
Chapter III, pp. 109-20, for a fuller discussion of Tou Ngo's death.)

As has been pointed out, Tou Ngo is seen in this play as "going
through the whole gamut of human emotions."[19] These emotions are
successfully conveyed by arias that are sometimes vaguely suggestive
and sometimes rather daringly explicit for Yüan drama. The first
aria assigned to Tou Ngo as a young widow (as a seven-year-old she was
given one line in the "wedge" or prologue) contains a veiled attack on
Heaven:

> Of my heart full of sorrow,
> Of my years of suffering,
> Is Heaven aware?
> If Heaven only knew my situation,
> Would it not also grow thin?

(YCH, p. 1501)[20]

The "years of suffering" and the "heart full of sorrow" refer, of course, to the hardship of Tou Ngo's widowhood; it appears all the more "unfair" when this happens to someone who lost her mother at the age of three and was separated from her father at seven. It is this sense of "unfairness"--which is part of the meaning of the character yüan 寃 (rendered "injustice") in the title--that prompts Tou Ngo's mild protest, even before Donkey Chang thrusts himself upon her. As yet her calls on Heaven are low-pitched and subdued, showing resignation as well as great restraint.

As her situation worsens--thanks to the schemes of Donkey Chang--and she is soon to be beheaded, Tou Ngo's complaints become more shrill and she clashes with Heaven head-on:

端正好 Tuan-cheng-hao

For no reason, I am found guilty by Imperial law;
Unexpectedly, I suffer punishment.
My cry of injustice startles Heaven and Earth!
In a moment, my drifting soul goes to Yama's Palace.
Why shouldn't I blame Heaven and Earth?

滾繡球 Kun hsiu-ch'iu

The sun and moon hang aloft by day and by night;
Ghosts and spirits hold power over our lives and deaths.
Heaven and Earth should distinguish the pure from
        the foul;
But how they have mixed up Bandit Chih and Yen Yüan![*]
The good suffer poverty and short life;
The wicked enjoy wealth, nobility, and long life.
Even Heaven and Earth have come to fear the strong
        and oppress the weak.
They, after all, only push the boats following the
        current.
Oh Earth, as you fail to discriminate between good
        and evil,
        How can you function as Earth?

---

* "[Both] were of the Spring and Autumn period. [Bandit Chih] was a notorious robber; and [Yen Yüan], a Confucian disciple, was a virtuous person who died young in poverty (Historical Records, chüan 61, p. 8b). Later these two persons represented the extreme good and bad."--Shih (I), p. 191.

> Oh Heaven, in mistaking the sage and the fool,
> You are called Heaven in vain!

(<u>YCH</u>, p. 1509)[21]

Characterizing the direct, undisguised attack this time is an unbending, even indignant sense of moral righteousness, at once noble and forceful. Joined by sun, moon, day, night, ghosts, and spirits, the images of Heaven and Earth continue to dominate. These and other cosmic images in the play (such as snow, water, drought) transcend (while still being related to) the personal suffering of a lone woman and move onto a universal plane.[22] Furthermore, they bring to the fore the confrontation between good and evil. In Tou Ngo's mind, not only have the elements abandoned their proper office of upholding justice; they have even conspired with evil against good (which is equated with innocence). By accusing nature itself, Tou pits herself against the whole universe. It is a confrontation in which she is not given much of a chance, to be sure; yet she emerges from it a much taller and greater figure than a plain, helpless woman--on the strength of her moral courage. As she gains considerably in stature as a tragic character, so does the play as a testimony to the human potential dignity and nobility. The poetic language has done a splendid job for the mechanism of the play. (See also the section on the convention of a single singing role [Chapter III, pp. 109-20], where the relationship between lyrics and the characterization of Tou Ngo is studied at greater length.)

The use of spoken verse appears to be selective and frugal. In the <u>YCH</u> version, there are only two major versified speeches in the entire play, assigned to Lu the physician and Tou Ngo's father, respectively.[23] Only the former is examined here. The piece comes at the beginning of Act II, when the physician makes his second appearance:

> Physician by profession am I.
> Patients I have treated have been known to die,
> But complaints from those who passed away
> Have never closed my doors for half a day.

> Hard by there lives a certain Madam Ts'ai.
> Some twenty silver taels I owed
> This hag. The more importunate she became,
> The more it fanned my anger's flame--
> Till I set upon her on a lonely road.
> There, two meddlers happened by

Raising such a hue and cry:
"murder foul in broad daylight!"

I dropped my rope and fled in fright.
Nothing happened all that night,
But my wits had all been shaken
And my conscience did awaken:

Human life's the thing of greatest worth,
The prime concern of Heaven and Earth.
Physician no longer, I will lead
A new life to change my karma. And I'll read
A passage from the sutras for those dead
Whose sad, untimely ends are on my head.

(YCH, p. 1504)

The tone of this verse is a mixture of levity and seriousness. In fact, it starts out on a distinctly lighthearted note and ends with unmistakable gravity, indicating the change of moral outlook in Doctor Lu. The first stanza harks back to his entrance piece in Act I,

I diagnose disease with care,
And prescribe according to the medicine book.
I cannot bring dead men back to life,
But the live ones by my doctoring often die.

(YCH, p. 1500)[24]

which is also characterized by a certain mischievous cheerfulness.

The next stanza is basically a recapitulation of Doctor Lu's earlier, thwarted murder attempt. Yet it is different, and supplies more facts. To compare, here is the incident:

Lu: Madam, I have no money at home. Come with me to the village, and I shall get the money for you.

Ts'ai: I shall go with you.

(They start walking.)

Lu [aside]: Well, here we are--nobody to the east, nobody to the west. If I don't do the job here, what am I waiting for? I have some rope with me. [Turning to Ts'ai.] Hey, Mistress, who is calling you?

Ts'ai: Where?

(Doctor Lu tries to strangle her. Old Chang and Donkey Chang
rush forward; Doctor Lu hurries away. . . .)

(YCH, p. 1500)[25]

Whereas the acted-out scene is objectively presented, the recounting
offers a version strictly from the Doctor's point of view; the former is
detached, the latter involved. What was in the first instance an unim-
passioned line of stage direction--"Old Chang and Donkey Chang rush
forward"--is transformed in the second into an audible visualization:
"There, two meddlers happened by/Raising such a hue and cry:/'Murder
foul in broad daylight!'" The recapitulation is not a meaningless repetition, but a lively enhancement.

The third stanza picks up the story where the previous scene
leaves off--"Doctor Lu hurries away"--and succinctly sums up the
impact of the incident on the quack. It marks the transition of tone
from carefreeness to solemnity, a transition that parallels the trans-
formation of Doctor Lu's personality from one of frivolous irresponsi-
bility to being religiously introspective.

The weightiness that is being built up culminates in the last
stanza, with the overt moral that "Human life's the thing of greatest
worth,/The prime concern of Heaven and Earth." Here, again, reference to heaven and earth in conjunction with human lives is made,
consistent with their use in the intense lyrics sung by Tou Ngo, portions of which we have seen. The picture of seriousness is complete
when such religious entities as karma and sutra are conjured up to lend
their weight. That the physician should learn about the value of human
lives after these years of practice--or malpractice--and that the erst-
while murderer should turn preacher of the sacredness of life are just
fine examples of the many-forked irony that the playwright seems fond
of and skilled in. In short, the verse recited by Doctor Lu contains
various kinds of messages, light and heavy, all contributing to the
audience's understanding of and response to the drama.

The Less-Than-Greats

The Gold Phoenix Hairpins

Unlike Injustice to Tou Ngo or The Mo-ho-lo Doll, Cheng T'ing-
yü's The Gold Phoenix Hairpins is, on balance, light and humorous.

The play features the ups and downs of Scholar Chao, whose own undoing--
as well as eventual redemption--is his generosity and human kindness.
Several times his nobility brings him to the brink of disaster, and each
time it pulls him through. So the play dramatizes the time-honored
dictum, "As ye sow, so shall ye reap." On the surface, it conforms to
the formula of judgment reversal, serving up poetic justice just before
the final curtain. Yet, significantly, there is no exploitation of the trial
scenes in this play, unlike Injustice or Doll, for instance. As a matter
of fact, both trials in Hairpins are haphazardly done: no courtrooms,
no professional judges (good or bad), no conflict of interest between the
plaintiff and the defendant, no direct jibe at venal and hollow-headed
officialdom, and so on. Even the working out of justice is initiated, not
by judges or anyone close to the system, but by an innkeeper. The focus
of this play seems to lie in another direction.

The clue to this focus is language. Throughout the play, Scholar
Chao speaks like a pedant. Never satisfied (or so it appears) with plain,
straightforward speech, he always talks (sings) obliquely, constantly
making historical or literary allusions which are in turn obvious or ambiguous, pertinent or irrelevant. The effect is two-fold. On one hand,
the erudition he exhibits may be taken as the credentials of a scholar who
finishes first in the imperial examination. On the other hand, the bookish
cant underscores Chao's incapacity to deal realistically with workaday
life; mentally, he dwells in a realm far from the madding (or even sanity-
producing) crowd. Capitalizing on the incompatibility between his supposedly admirable learning and his pitiful inability to cope with reality,
the play is more a satire on the Confucian scholar (ju 儒) than an advocacy of Confucian ethics. And Scholar Chao's pedantic language plays a
part in the lightness and humor that animate the drama.

An ill-starred student, Chao's acknowledged scholarship does not
get him anywhere. True, everything seems rosy for a moment when he
has placed first in the examination and is even appointed to an official
post. The rosiness evaporates, however, when it is announced that the
Sage Presence has revoked the appointment because Chao has inadvertently caused the displeasure of His Majesty. Chao's reaction to this
sudden blow is indicative of his approach and attitude to almost all
worldly affairs:

(sings)   那吒令 Na-cha ling

My devotion to study equalled that of the mat-cutting
          Kuan Ning,[1]

---

[1] Kuan Ning, of the Age of the Three Kingdoms, "used to study on the

48

My diligence matched that of the wall-drilling
 K'uang Heng,[2]
My perseverance compared to that of the food-begging
 Han Hsin.[3]
The lesser scholars, the underlings--
None of them would "follow the examples of the
 virtuous."[4]

(says)

Such has been my lot!

(sings)   崔踏枝 Ch'üeh t'a-chih

Taking off the purple robe of silk,
I put on my garment of old.
A long, long way I had gone,
In a sad, sad mood I now return.
How the entire thing resembles the dream of Chiang
 Yen:[5]

(says)

When I get home, my wife'll surely ask me about
 the job.

---

same mat with Hua Hsin, but when Hua left his seat to take a peep
at the carriages of high officials passing by, Kuan cut the mat in
two and sat separate." See CW.

[2] CW quotes Hsi-ching tsa-chi 西京雜記: "K'uang was diligent but
could not afford a candle. . . . , so he drilled through the wall and
studied by the light that came from the next-door neighbor through
the hole."

[3] The story of the Great General of Han was so popular that it formed
the basis of at least one Yüan play, attributed to Wang Chung-wen.
See Huang.

[4] Confucian Analects, IV, Legge, p. 170.

[5] A famed poet in his time, Chiang once dreamed of a man who told
him, "For many years I have left my pen with you. It's time you
returned it." Chiang reached into his pocket, produced a five-
colored pen, and returned it as demanded. From then on he could
no longer write a single good line. See CW.

(sings)

I can see her now, demanding a divorce.

寄生草　Chi-sheng ts'ao

All scholars under heaven have ambitions
Even if their learning is only superficial.
Thousands intend to make good,
But nine out of ten are frustrated.
Since P'an-ku[6] created the world, no scholars
    have been known to be well-off;
Who knows how many of Confucius' disciples[7]
    were poverty-stricken?

(WP, p. 186)

His erudition being of the proverbial sort, there is nothing recondite or
profound in Chao's speech; but seven allusions at a clip cannot but produce at least the appearance of learnedness. The allusions here are all
pertinent and make good sense. By comparing himself with historical
figures known for their extraordinary single-mindedness in pursuit of
their goals (allusions 1 through 3), Chao tells us his own story and
avails himself of the sympathy and respect generally accorded these
figures. The phrase from Confucian Analects (4) sounds trite--but
perhaps appropriately so. The reference to Chiang Yen's dream poign-
antly alludes to his own short-lived moment of glory and success. But
if Chao's voice is bitter at the beginning, his bitterness is not directed
toward anyone or anything in particular. In point of fact, he is quick to
rationalize his less-than-pleasant personal experience; after all, he
reasons, it can happen to anybody (6 and 7). Even here, the scholar
betrays his tendency to take refuge in the past when it is the present he
has to face.

The tendency becomes more and more apparent as the play unfolds.
The next scene shows Scholar Chao returning home, empty-handed, to
face a disappointed and understandably concerned wife:

Wife (says): If you don't find yourself an employer and
    earn a living, how are we to survive?

---

[6] Fabled creator of the universe.

[7] Traditionally estimated at three thousand.

Chao (sings):   金盞兒   Chin chan-erh

> One could wear all the hide off his body
> Before he could find a patron in these days.
> No more do men believe "all men are brothers";[1]
>   and besides,
> "The crooked are advanced, the upright dismissed"[2]
>   in the court.
> I might as well point to a flying goose and declare
>   it my meal,[3]
> Or earn a living by catching the moon in the water.[4]
> It would be like Master Lü visiting his acquaintance
>   of old,[5] or
> Like Wu Wen-cheng looking for a bosom friend.[6]

(WP, p. 187)

Again, Chao rationalizes in his pedantic manner, crowding his indirect statements with allusions. And again, the allusions persuade us that he is never likely to succeed in the world of affairs. Worse still, he flees even before the battle is joined, retreating to the ivory towers of yesteryear where he feels at home and from which he can hurl down proverbs against the besieging forces of reality. One soon begins to wonder if the whole question of the pertinency of Chao's references is not, after

---

[1] Confucian Analects, XII, Legge, p. 253.

[2] Confucian Analects, II, Legge, p. 152.

[3] The source is not known to me, but its message is obvious.

[4] There are at least two possible sources. One legend has it that Li Po, the great T'ang poet, drowned himself in an attempt to catch the moon in the water. The Buddhist classics also refer to this life as the illusory reflection of the moon in the water. But, again, the phrase's meaning is self-apparent.

[5] Possibly alluding to Lü An, whose visit to Chi K'ang when the latter was not home gave rise to the phrase "Lü An t'i-feng" 呂安題鳳 [Lü An writes the character "phoenix" on the door]. The story is found in Shih-shuo hsin-yü. See CW.

[6] The allusion is not known to me.

all, beside the point: maybe the important thing here is simply to recognize Scholar Chao's apparently irrepressible wish to identify with comforting historical personages and events--regardless of their relevance.

The suspicion is confirmed before long. With his wife, his child, and his landlord the Innkeeper prodding all the time, Chao finally decides on the trade he knows best: he will sell poems on Choubridge where "numerous people come and go." The scholar has already concluded a transaction and netted two hundred coppers when Tiger Li, the villain, and Judge Chang, dressed as a low official, <u>ku</u> (though he says he is "just a rustic" chuang-nung 莊農) run into each other on the bridge. What ensues is so illuminating of our point that it is worth quoting at some length:

Li (<u>grabs Chang</u>): Well met! You borrowed two hundred from me. Why haven't you paid it back?

Chang: Brother, I'm just an old farmer who is new to this city. . . . Forgive me, brother, for bumping into you.

Li: You owe me two hundred and refuse to return it. Let's jump into the river.

Chang: Brother, you've mistaken me for someone else! I don't owe you any money!

Li: You do too! All right, you won't pay me back. Well, let's jump into the river and settle it that way. (<u>He grabs Chang and is ready to jump.</u>)

Chang: Hold! Spare me, brother! Would you kill a man for money? Human life concerns both heaven and earth! If it's money you want, I can borrow two hundred for you.

Li: All I ask is my money back.

Chang: Alas for me! If only some passer-by would come and intervene.

Chao (<u>says</u>): I have no sooner got a customer than they start a quarrel here. I'll have to be the peacemaker.

(<u>sings</u>)   石榴花 <u>Shih-liu hua</u>

Look at them, pushing and shoving each other;
They'll never listen to me.

That one, menacing-looking, brandishes his arms
and fists with anger intense.

(says)

My respects to you, brother. Please don't do the deed!

Li: He won't pay back my two hundred, so I'm going to
take him into the river with me.

Chao (sings):

The more he's cajoled, the tougher he gets.

Chang: Brother, if you would let me go, I'd find the
money for you. (He greets Scholar Chao.) My
respects, brother. Thank you for intervening.
I see you have two hundred coppers. Would you
lend it to me so I can pay him off. --I'll return the
sum with one hundred percent interest. I really
couldn't help bumping into this footpad, you know!

Li: Watch your language! You owed me money.

Chao (sings):

Ai, you're Lord Meng-ch'ang who supported ruffians in his house.[1]

Chang: Brother, what's your name?

Li: I am Tiger Li.

Chao (sings):

And you are Yen P'ing-chung so skilled in human
relations.[2]
One who wouldn't do a cock-crow at Han-ku Pass,[3]

---

[1] Lord Meng-ch'ang, of the Warring State Period, is known for his
generous and indiscriminate hospitality toward anyone who would
stay with him. Cf. Shih Chi 史記 [Historical Records], 75.

[2] Confucian Analects, V, Legge, p. 179. Yen P'ing-chung was of
the Spring and Autumn Period. Whether he was "so skilled in human
relationship," however, is not clear from his biography. Cf. Shih
Chi, 62.

[3] According to Shih Chi, 75, a retainer of Lord Meng-ch'ang imitated

Yet for want of money you would leap from Choubridge.

鬪鵪鶉 Tou an-ch'un

It seems now your patron is in danger, [4]
And now is the time to return T'ien-wen's favor.[5]
You there--don't worry as if you were Li Mi;[6]
And you--please do as Po Tang did and set him
 free.[7]

Li: Not until he returns the money.

Chao (sings):

Ai: You're as cross as Chou Yü visiting Lu Su,[8]
Menacingly keeping hold of his belt.
If I don't intercede--I've already made a fool of
 myself by getting involved;
But if I do, yet one more person will be in trouble!

(WP, pp. 188-89)

Here can be seen the sharp contrast between the imminence of the
business at hand--with its potential grave consequences--and the Oxford
don manner with which Scholar Chao handles it. The incongruity, which
is the source of all that is mildly comic and humorous in this play, is
further magnified or compounded by the fact that most of Chao's allusions

---

a rooster's crow one night when his Lord wanted desperately to get
through the pass. The guards, hearing the crow, thought daybreak
had come and opened the gate for them.

[4] Cf. (3).

[5] T'ien Wen is the name of Lord Meng-ch'ang.

[6] There are three Li Mi's listed in CW; it is not clear which one and
and what deed this alludes to.

[7] The allusion is not clear to me. It appears in at least one other
tsa-chü, Ts'un lo t'ang 村樂堂, WP, p. 912.

[8] Chou, of the Age of Three Kingdoms, was known to be of choleric
temperament.

bear scarcely at all on the critical situation. If anything, the predatory relationship between Tiger Li and Judge Chang is as far as one can get from the relationship between Lord Meng-ch'ang and his retainers. It appears that Scholar Chao just rattles off his allusions, doing his best to delay the moment when he finally has to act. Eventually, Chao gives Tiger Li all he has and rescues Judge Chang--and it is this good deed, not his erudition, that finally brings him good fortune at the play's end.

Hairpins, it appears to me, should be read as a mockery of the impractical Confucian scholar. This thesis becomes the more plausible when Judge Chang recites--with tongue in cheek, most likely--the last words of the play:

> Devoted scholar who burns midnight oil
> Craves the Sage's favor in the Heavenly Palace.
> What ten long years of study failed to achieve
> Was got by investing only two hundred coppers.

(WP, p. 201)

Scholar-bureaucrats who are minor characters are not infrequently made farcical on the Chinese stage,[26] but in Hairpins Scholar Chao has the singing role and the mockery here is of a higher level than farce, infinitely subtler and more sophisticated--largely because of the contribution of language on all levels.

Rescue of a Filial Son

Its title notwithstanding,[27] Wang Chung-wen's Rescue of the Filial Son features, in fact, a noble, loving mother. Mrs. Yang, a widow, allows Hsing-tsu, her elder son, to be conscripted while retaining Hsieh-tsu, the younger. When Ch'un-hsiang, Hsing-tsu's wife, is recalled by her family, the young Hsieh-tsu escorts her through most of the journey. Soon after she is left on her own, a scurrilous quack doctor abducts her by force. Ch'un-hsiang's mother files a suit against Hsieh-tsu for the alleged murder of his sister-in-law, presumably after a thwarted attempt to seduce her. Mrs. Yang turns into a fearless champion to defend the honor and life of her son. She has to fight not only the in-law-turned-plaintiff, but virtually the entire judicial system which insists on a swift conclusion instead of careful examination of the case.

When the play begins, Prefect Wang has just arrived for the express purpose of drafting soldiers: one of the two Yang brothers has to be conscripted. But which one?

> Wang: You, ma'am, you have two sons. Which one is to be the soldier?

> Mrs. Yang: Please, your honor, dismount your horse and come to our humble home. My two sons--you may choose either one.

> Yang: Well, during my recruiting mission so far, I haven't had a moment's rest. Now you ask me to go to your place to rest a while and choose either one of your two sons--all right, I'll do that: I have nothing to fear.

(YCH, p. 758; emphasis mine)

Through the use of repetition, the otherwise inconsequential dialogue between the prefect and the mother raises, in effect, the issue of which of the two sons is to go. At this juncture, Mrs. Yang's stance seems an impartial one; significantly, her reply that either may go is reiterated by the prefect. A second question immediately arises: if this is the case, why does Mrs. Yang take the trouble of inviting the prefect to her house? The repetition and the number game in the quoted passage generates a bit of interest.

The interest is sustained and capitalized on in the ensuing scene. When the prefect names Hsieh-tsu, the younger of the two, as his choice, Mrs. Yang can no longer maintain her masked impartiality; instead, she insists that Hsing-tsu, the elder, is better cut out for soldiering. Her insistence is so strong--she repeats four times, including once in an aria, that Hsieh-tsu is "too frail" to make a soldier--that it angers the prefect, who becomes suspicious:

Wang: Come now! which one is going?

Mrs. Yang: The elder is stronger--he shall go. The younger is too weak to go.

Wang: Oh? So you're saying that the elder, stronger, may go, and the younger, being weak, may not?

Mrs. Yang: Truly, the younger may not.

Wang: Silence, old woman! You told me I could choose

eitherone of your two sons. . . . The elder one
must be your step-son, for whom you do not care
too much, and the younger must be your own flesh.
As the saying goes, "It is easier to give your
worldly goods to one of your own flesh." That must
be why you won't let him go.

(recites)

Scheming, this hag, and sly!
She would dupe me before my very eye,
Insisting I take the older one
Who must be her step-son.

(says)

You old woman! Your explanation had better be
good; otherwise. . . . Chang Ch'ien [his servant],[28]
have the heavy cudgels ready!

(YCH, pp. 758-59)

Again, there are a lot of repetitions, and again they sharpen the audience's focus of interest and steadily build up a kind of tension that culminates in the prefect's doggerel (which is essentially a recapitulation).

The tension is resolved when Mrs. Yang's explanation comes, as
a surprise to the prefect and, for that matter, the audience. True, she
says, one of her sons was by the concubine of her husband, but that one
is the younger, Hsieh-tsu, whom she has been trying to shield from
harm. She goes on to present her case,

Why, your honor asks, do I [choose to send away]
the elder? Well, because he's my own. And should
anything happen to him, I shall still have the younger
one around to take care of my old age.--For they
say, and I'm sure your honor would agree, "No
prince leaves a banquet but he's full or drunk; no
soldier leaves the battlefield but he's wounded or
dead." If I send the younger away and something
happens to him, I'd hold myself responsible. And
I shall be ashamed to face my husband [who entrusted
him to me] in the underworld. . . .

(YCH, p. 759)

As curiosity, roused by the use of repetition, and the ensuing tension
come to a satisfactory finale, the sensitivity and nobility of Mrs. Yang
is established beyond doubt. It is these qualities that gain her the
audience's sympathy and respect even when, later on, her defense of
Hsieh-tsu borders on arrogance.

The device is not always successful; the sets of repetitions that
closely follow are half-failures at best. Preparing to leave home,
Hsing-tsu hands his wife a sword, intending it as a gift for her brother,
but Ch'un-hsiang hesitates to accept it:

> Ch'un-hsiang: Husband, does mother know this?
>
> Hsing-tsu: No.
>
> Ch'un-hsiang: And your brother?
>
> Hsing-tsu: Nor he.
>
> Ch'un-hsiang: Are you not too indiscreet, husband?
> You give me this sword without mother or brother
> knowing it. Later, if they see my brother carrying
> it, they might accuse me of stealing the Yangs'
> property.

(<u>YCH</u>, p. 759)

The sound of their argument catches the attention of the others, who
demand to know what it is about. The dialogue, in virtually the same
words, is then reported <u>twice</u> by Ch'un-hsiang, to Mrs. Yang and
Prefect Wang, respectively. Much impressed by Ch'un-hsiang's pru-
dence and honesty, Wang encourages her to do as her husband bids,
adding, "If there be any dispute in the future, you may call me as witness. This sword--some day I may be <u>your</u> key witness!" (<u>YCH</u>,
p. 760)

As the play develops, it becomes obvious that the repetition here
is an attempt to underscore the importance of the sword, which does
ironically turn up as a piece of evidence against Hsieh-tsu in the legal
case. But even without the device, the murder trials would have gone
the same way--with the same results. There is evident irony on the
part of Prefect Wang, to be sure, when, as judge of the second trial,
he recognizes the sword (<u>YCH</u>, p. 772); but that is about all it effects.
The relatively insignificant role assigned to the sword later in the play
does not justify the emphasis placed on it in this incident. The

audience's expectation, raised high at the signal of repetition, is never fully met.

These two instances of repeating--one successful, the other somewhat non sequitur and lame--are indicative of the overall unevenness of Rescue's language on the prose and verse levels. In the fourth act, a great deal of prose has to be used to tie up several loose ends; in fact, the first aria is not sung until the act is well past midway. Right in the middle of that long, fatiguing portion of prose, however, a piece of verse, given to Hsieh-tsu, is inserted (YCH, pp. 772-73). It runs for forty-eight lines--perhaps as long as any verse recapitulation to be found in the entire tsa-chü repertoire, and certainly the longest in the judgment reversal group. In addition to its regular functions, the verse's existence offers variety in a predominantly "prosaic" context. Because it is substantially long, the verse stands out and minimizes the disadvantage of monotony. It also modulates the unbridled pace of action that results from the abundant use of dialog. The handling of Hsieh-tsu's verse may thus be deemed a technical success.

Unfortunately, however, the "plus" is immediately negated by a "minus." Hsieh-tsu's moving recital prompts the prefect to make a long-winded speech, in which he declares, among other things, that

> Although the intention of the law is now obscure, it can still be inferred by observing human feelings. The tears of the suspect of a serious crime fall on the cangue and then drop onto the ground, reaching Hades. There, a certain Weed of Bitterness grows, bearing a seed the size of a wu-t'ung seed. It is so hard that neither swords nor axes can break it. That is the way the fair and impartial heaven and earth respond and reveal themselves. . . .

> (YCH, p. 773)

Given the context, the conceit of "the Weed of Bitterness" and its seed seem farfetched at best, as are Prefect Wang's similes (of pot and furnace) ranted out in the same breath (YCH, p. 773).[29]

But if the quality of prose and verse in Rescue seems uneven, that of its arias is consistently maintained. Except in the first act, where she is treated as a rather conventional woman, the prevailing tone of Mrs. Yang's arias is one of defiance and self-assurance. In the second act, Ch'un-hsiang's mother, mistaking a rotted corpse for her missing daughter's, has just filed a suit against Hsieh-tsu; Mrs. Yang is requested to identify the corpse:

Clerk: Old woman, is this [Ch'un-hsiang's] corpse?

Mrs. Yang (sings): 倘秀才 T'ang hsiu-ts'ai

The face has been pecked by crows or magpies,
The feet bitten off by wolves or hounds:
I cannot be too careful--if this be my child. . . .

Judge: We'd best flog her.

Mrs. Yang (sings):

Don't get mad, your honor,
Don't take offense, good clerk:
Allow me to offer my considered view. . . .

Clerk: Old woman! Someone was murdered and you're taking time to offer your considered view!

Mrs. Yang (sings):

So-called cases of murder often turn out to be
otherwise.

Clerk: I'm determined to investigate and make a successful case out of this one. . . .

Mrs. Yang (sings):

Then proceed with your investigation slowly;
don't rush things.
Examine scrupulously
Interrogate thoroughly
For fear you may leave a shade of ambiguity.

Clerk: But I am the chief clerk. . . .

Mrs. Yang (sings):

Then don't abuse the authority of your office.

Clerk: This pen of mine can kill. . . .

Mrs. Yang (sings):

Then don't trifle with its power.

Clerk: My pen is sharper than the knife. . . .

Mrs. Yang (sings):

> Sharper than a knife it may be; so remember
> When someone is killed by it, he is dead forever.
> Only after its bell has chimed
> Are we aware of the temple's existence in the
>   mountain;
> Only after we have reached the other bank
> Do we realize the village has been isolated
>   by water.
> Therefore: be careful not to misjudge the
>   innocent!

(<u>YCH</u>, p. 765)

It should be pointed out that Mrs. Yang, of all the "victimized" characters in the judgment reversal plays, is the only one to fight courageously to the end for what she believes. The belief is a mother's blind faith in her son; the courage comes from a mother's resoluteness to defend her young. It is a simple process through which a conventional mother is transformed into a brave champion of justice--justice as she understands it. (Her performance is made more moving and admirable by the fact that Hsieh-tsu is but her step-son.) If Mrs. Yang's arias, like the one shown above, often ring with self-righteousness,[30] it merely reflects a soul humble but sure of itself, loving, and dignified.

When all available evidence points to Hsieh-tsu as the culprit, Mrs. Yang becomes the single stumbling block between the court clerk and his goal "to make a successful [murder] case out of this one." In spite of the clerk's constant, unnerving pressure, she refuses to identify the corpse as her daughter-in-law:

(sings)　　　　　刀刀令 Tao-tao ling

> This case involving both heaven and human life
> Now rests in your hands.
> But how can I, as close kin, identify this corpse
> When no autopsy has been conducted?
>
> The rainy season is here
> With all its summer heat.
> The corpse has disintegrated,
> The home of maggots and worms.
> Indeed I cannot identify it,

Indeed I cannot recognize it!
Nothing about it looks as I remember her.

(YCH, p. 765)

The defiant note established here in the second act runs throughout the
rest of the play. It is noteworthy that even in times of panic and great
confusion, Mrs. Yang manages to keep a cool head; there is reason in
her madness. Her reason and madness prove frustrating to the clerk,
but they cannot change his mind; and yet, they are not wasted either,
for they succeed in delaying the execution of Hsieh-tsu--which is what
really counts--until the arrival of Prefect Wang and the return of Hsing-
tsu together with Ch'un-hsiang, safe and sound.

The Chalk Circle

The Chalk Circle,[31] by Li Hsing-tao, is a drama in which weighty
seriousness alternates with light-minded frivolity. Its plot comprises
a succession of dark events, in turn gloomy, horrible, outrageous, or
solemn. Mrs. Ma, who is herself having an affair with Clerk Chao,
goads her husband into believing that Hai-t'ang, his concubine, is un-
faithful to him. After giving Hai-t'ang a good beating, Mr. Ma himself
dies of poison administered by his legal wife through a clever scheme.
(Act I.) Hai-t'ang, however, is charged with the hideous deed. The
case is brought to the court where Clerk Chao serves as the de facto
judge; predictably, Hai-t'ang suffers all manner of torture until a
deposition acknowledging the criminal act is extracted from her. (Act II.)
She is then shown trudging, in cangue and fetters, in a heavy snowstorm
on her way to K'ai-feng to be sentenced. (Act III.) There, a second trial
is held and, with the Solomon's Judgment of the chalk circle, Judge Pao
is able to uncover the truth. (Act IV.)

The heavy links in this chain of events are greatly lightened by
the playwright's adroit maneuvering with prose and verse; comic elements are timely introduced to dispel much of the sobriety and grim-
ness. These interludes are evenly distributed throughout the play. The
ribald, shameless confessions of Mrs. Ma and Clerk Chao in Act I
touch off the theme of "appearance and reality." The second act brings
forth jokes on officialdom in addition to lines of a bawdy nature. In
Act III, the coarseness and vulgarity of the tavern owner's entrance
verse qualify it for admission into the mainstream of obscenity. The
last act concludes, significantly, with the two shameless adulterers

badmouthing each other, betraying the true nature of their affair. Thus, except for a couple of jibes aimed at the bureaucracy, the majority of the verbal railleries or jests form a network centering on the lowly, lewd, and lustful.

Even the exception turns out to be not so exceptional. After all, scurrilities directed at "those above" are such a common--in fact, regular--feature in courtroom plays that it may well have been considered part of the convention. (More on this in the next chapter, pp. 99-103.) In Circle, Prefect Su Shun enters with a doggerel quatrain:

> Although a judge, of laws
> I'm plainly ignorant;
> But he who offers me silver
> Shall be acquitted innocent.

(YCH, p. 1116)

He also has an exit piece, complete with, as it were, a preface:

(says)

> The case is concluded. Come to think of it, I did
> not make any decision, even though I am in charge.
> Everything, including whether the defendant should
> be flogged or dismissed, rested with the power of
> Clerk Chao. Am I just a fool?

(recites)

> Whoever the court may falsely arraign
> I'll accept the judgment and not complain;
> They may do what they wish--foul or fair,
> Just so I get my agreed-upon share.

(YCH, p. 1120)

The overall tone of both verses is not unlike that of, say, the entrance verse recited by the comic Prefect-Judge in The Mo-ho-lo Doll, quoted on an earlier occasion:

> When I'm the judge I hear each plea
> With fine impartiality
> I take my gold with an open mind
> From defense and plaintiff equally.

The senior judge would (if he knew)
Flog me till the cocks all crew.

(YCH, p. 1375)[32]

So, in one form or another, this type of self-mockery by office-holders
occurs in most judgment reversal plays (see above, p. 39ff).

But then Prefect Su in Circle is something else again. Unlike his
counterparts in other plays who are clearly flat characters, he has for-
mulated a distinct and somewhat unorthodox view of bureaucracy. After
reciting the entrance piece, he goes on to tell the audience in what
appears to be a pensive, philosophical manner:

> Just because I'm soft-headed or soft-hearted, the ungrate-
> ful populace here in Cheng-chou have insultingly called me
> by the soubriquet of "Soft Su."[33] It has spread far and wide.
>
> But I have known quite a few able and smart officials
> who abuse their authority and bring many a family to ruin.
> On the other hand, who knows how many lives a soft per-
> son like myself must have preserved unknown to others?

(YCH, p. 1116)

Corrupt bureaucrats audacious and brazen enough to confess their
wrongdoings and lack of character are a regular feature of Yüan tsa-
chü, but one who impudently comes up with a theory rationalizing his
conduct--or misconduct--is a rarity. This departure from the norm,
together with his "preface" to the exit verse, lends Prefect Su an introspective image--something that sets him apart from the other, somewhat shallowly portrayed, officials. While still belonging to the convention, he has the appearance of being unconventional--perhaps deliberately made so by the playwright.

So much for the "exceptional" case. The obscene lines on which
the comedy of this play depends begin as soon as the first act opens
(following a short "prologue"):

(Enter Mrs. Ma.)

Mrs. Ma (recites):

> My countenance leaves a lot to be desired
> Although most people praise its color;

The powders and rouge washed off my face
Would supply a beauty parlor!

(says)

I'm Mr. Ma's legal wife.--He has a concubine,
by the name of, er, Hai-t'ang, I believe. They
have a child, now five years old.--And there's my
Clerk Chao, a jolly handsome fellow; and he has
a line of goods as long as a donkey's! We have an
amorous relationship. . . .

(YCH, pp. 1108-09)

Mrs. Ma's piece contains two important messages. The verse part
calls attention to the discrepancy between her two faces--one powdered,
the other real; and here is where the theme of appearance and reality
first suggests itself. The ensuing revelation, in the monologue, of her
extramarital sexual activity underscores her character as essentially
licentious and voluptuary. Both messages are echoed and reinforced
throughout the rest of the play. For example, when Clerk Chao enters,
he recites:

A clerk who loves his drink am I,
And with his neighbors' wives would lie.
But only she with the painted face
Holds in my heart the securest place!

(YCH, p. 1109)

The frivolity toward wanton sexual indulgence expressed in these lines
finds its counterpart in Mrs. Ma. They are a perfect pair--although
probably not a match made in heaven.

When Mrs. Ma unveils her plot to poison her husband, an overjoyed Clerk Chao exclaims, "You're not just some harlot that I chanced
to meet: I adore you as I would my mother" (YCH, p. 1109)! The
mention of "harlot" is significant, for Hai-t'ang, before she became
Mr. Ma's concubine, was a prostitute. Ironically, Hai-t'ang is the only
person in this play to evince any tender notion of love. Her romantic
tendency may be detected in such arias as Shang-hua-shih 賞花時 (in
the prologue), Tien chiang-ch'un 點絳唇 , and Hun-chiang lung 混江龍
(both in Act I). It must also be pointed out that the just quoted lascivious exchanges between Mrs. Ma and Clerk Chao are juxtaposed

with these arias which embody so much loftier and lovelier emotions.
Such an arrangement results in a contrast that again brings to the fore
the theme of appearance versus truth: Mrs. Ma, the lawful wife of Mr.
Ma, is in fact the shameless debaucher.

The vulgarities are sometimes kept up through indirect means.
For instance, commenting on her own scheme against Hai-t'ang, Mrs.
Ma is heard to recite:

> They say:
> Man may not intend to harm the tiger
> But the tiger is determined to wound him.
> I say:
> To fight a tiger--no man has the heart;
> But a timid tiger must make a meal of a fart.

> (YCH, p. 1115)

In these closing words of Act I, a proverb is altered to give it a scatological twist, and vulgarity is easily associated with the lewd and lustful.

While Mrs. Ma and Clerk Chao are rightfully the chief dispensers
of coarse jokes framed in irreverent language, they also get plenty of
help from other minor characters. A case in point is the court scene
in Act II, where the child is claimed by both Hai-t'ang and Mrs. Ma:

Hai-t'ang: Sir, you may ask the two grannies. They
ought to know the truth.

Chao: You, then. Tell me, whose child is this?

Granny Liu: I deliver seven or eight babies a day.
How can I remember something so many years
back?

Chao: The child is but five years old; it's not that long
ago. Just tell me whose it is.

Granny Liu: Well--that day in the delivery room, it
was as dark as pitch; you couldn't even see each
other's face. But I could tell by the feel of it that
the birth canal must have been Mrs. Ma's.

Chao: Nonsense! You, Granny Chang. Tell us.

66

Granny Chang: I remember the day they sent for me
  when the baby was going to have its first haircut.
  Mrs. Ma was holding the baby. I saw her breasts,
  white and sagging, like two big grain sacks, properly belonging to someone who'd been nursing a
  baby. Isn't it proof that it was Mrs. Ma's child?

(YCH, p. 1119)

The two grannies testify as expert witnesses, and they speak their professional jargon which enhances their credential as expert. The audience, however, could not have missed the bawdy overtones of the
speeches. Another instance is the entrance verse recited by the tavern
owner, with which the third act opens:

  Our service is fast, our wines impeccable;
  Clean and without dregs, unsurpassable.
  Next to the privy is the wine-vat shelter
  And the seat of my pants I use for a filter.

(YCH, p. 1121)

  Now, indelicate jokes with prurient implications are no novelty in
tsa-chü: their occasional appearance probably accounts for part of the
success of a vigorous, liberated language in a new genre full of vitality
and potential. However, only in Circle do they constitute a consistent
and massive assault--and achieve a calculated effect. For one thing,
these crude and anatomical allusions can be counted on to draw laughs
from the audience. Besides (and this seems equally important), they
are the yardstick by which the true nature of Mrs. Ma's affair with
Clerk Chao may be measured: after all, the style is the person.

  When the theme of appearance and reality is tied up in the final
act, the study of Mrs. Ma's and Clerk Chao's styles is complete. Judge
Pao's device of the chalk circle having successfully identified the true
mother (also a question involving the seeming and the truthful), he goes
on to pursue the illicit relationship between the two adulterers. It is
at this point that the image of the once "jolly handsome fellow" begins
to fall apart. In an effort to dissociate himself from Mrs. Ma, who is
now in trouble, Clerk Chao reasons with Judge Pao:

  Can't you see, your honor, the face of that woman is
  all smeared with powders? Wash them off and what's

left? Even if it was dropped on the road, I doubt anyone
would care to pick it up! Me? to sleep with her? Never!

to which "that woman" retorts:

> When we were alone, you used to say I was as beautiful
> as Kuan-yin, Goddess of Mercy. And now you denounce
> me and insult me like this. Oh, you heartless double-
> talker you!

(<u>YCH</u>, p. 1128)

Stripped of their masks, these great lovers can be seen for what they
really are. Desperately trying to save his own skin, Clerk Chao turns
into a coward, an antilover; as a last resort, he presents his case as
cogently as only an experienced and skillful attorney can:

> Since the woman and I have been carrying on for some
> time now, mine is a case of fornication at most, and I
> have no fear of death penalty.--I should know the laws.
>
> As to the poison: true, I did buy it, but it was not my
> idea. Besides, that woman put the poison in the soup
> that killed Lord Ma.
>
> As to her false claim of the child: I told her not to do
> so; but that woman insisted that the child would be a con-
> venient way to get at the legacy of Lord Ma.
>
> Now, I am a poor clerk, with no silver to spare. So,
> it was that woman who bribed the neighbors and the
> grannies [to bear false witnesses]. It was also that wo-
> man who induced the guards to make an attempt on Hai-
> t'ang's life on the road.

(<u>YCH</u>, p. 1129)

The presentation is effective--not so much in swaying Judge Pao as in
triggering more jeers and laughter (everyone loves to boo the villain).
In contrast, Mrs. Ma exhibits more courage, even in her clownish way:

> Fie on you, worthless beggar! You've said it all:
> what more can I add? So it's me, it's me! One death
> is as bad as another. And when we're dead, we can
> be husband and wife, forever: what comfort!

(<u>YCH</u>, p. 1129)

The Less Satisfactory Plays

In the last two sections we treated some judgment reversal plays in which language works well as an integral part of the drama it conveys. The playwright's handling of language on all levels is judged by the extent to which it measurably relates to theme, characterization, or structure-- or any combination of these. By contrast, the remaining two plays from our group--Kerchief and Child--appear weaker and inferior in the use of language. Unwarranted repetitions and verbal play that serve little or no dramatic purpose are their chief weaknesses.

Judgment on the Kerchief

In Lu Teng-shan's[34] Judgment on the Kerchief, Wang Hsiao-erh, a bum, gets himself entangled in a murder plot, but is eventually acquitted when a sympathetic and conscientious clerk intervenes and uncovers the truth. Wang's trouble starts when he breaks a commode belonging to the rich Liu family. A quarrel follows, and in no time heated, threatening language is exchanged:

> Mr. Liu: I'm rich and you're poor. So if I beat you to
> death, all I stand to lose is a few coppers.
>
> Wang: Oh yeah? If we meet on high street, I won't
> trouble you with so much as a word; but if we meet
> in the back alley, I'll kill you!
>
> Mrs. Liu: Listen to him talk! But what he has said
> he may well do. Demand from him a warranty
> of life. [To Wang.] If, within one hundred days,
> [Mr. Liu] should suffer from any headache or
> slight fever, you shall be held responsible. Be-
> yond one hundred days, you're free.

> (YCH, pp. 669-70)

And so Wang is obliged to become the warrantor for Mr. Liu's life. Mrs. Liu then conspires with her adulterer, a Taoist monk, murders her husband, and makes Wang a convenient scapegoat.

The "commode commotion" and its dialogue are repeated three times in the play, all in prose. The first repetition, made by Mrs. Liu to her lover in the "interlude" (wedge), closely follows the scene as presented in Act I, partially quoted above:

> The other day Wang Hsiao-erh broke a commode of ours,
> and Mr. Liu yelled a few words and said: "A rich man
> like me loses only a few coppers if he beats you to death!"
> And Wang Hsiao-erh retorted: "If I see you on high street,
> I won't trouble you with so much as a word; but if we meet
> in the back alley, I'll kill you!" And for that I extracted
> from him a life warranty. . . .

(<u>YCH</u>, p. 670)

The incident, in practically identical words, is summarized once again by Mrs. Liu at the first trial, when she accuses Wang of murdering her husband:

> Prefect: What's your complaint? Tell us!
>
> Mrs. Liu: I am Liu P'ing-yüan's wife. The other day,
> this Wang Hsiao-erh here broke a commode of ours.
> My husband quarreled with him and said: "A rich
> man like me loses only a few coppers if he beats you
> to death!" And Wang Hsiao-erh retorted: "If I see
> you on high street, I won't trouble you with so much
> as a word; but if we meet in the back alley, I'll kill
> you!" And so I demanded from him a life warranty. . . .

(<u>YCH</u>, p. 671)

Now, granting the significance of the incident as <u>causa sine qua non</u> for Wang's subsequent suffering, to repeat it twice in quick succession and without variation constitutes, to my mind, artistic blunder or carelessness. Not that recapitulations are uncommon in <u>tsa-chü</u>; quite the contrary, their occurrence on the Yüan stage is frequent, but most of them can be justified because they serve some dramatic purposes. As we have seen earlier, the recapitulation by Liu Yü-niang in <u>The Mo-ho-lo Doll</u>, done in orderly verse, is connected with the advent of justice, among other things (above, p. 40ff.). In <u>Injustice to Tou Ngo</u> also, Dr. Ts'ai's recounting his own foiled murder attempt, also offered in verse, not only provides a fresh, different point of view, but indicates a significant change in the outlook of an important--albeit minor--character (p. 44ff.). If Mrs. Liu's repetition were done, say, in a pseudo-elegant verse form, it might achieve an ironical effect because of contrast with the lowness of her character or the situation or both. Or, if she tried in her version to distort the truth, it might help display her personality better. As it stands, however, only redundancy results.

In comparison, the third repeat, by Wang Hsiao-erh, is a success. As he faces the second judge (in the third act), Wang has this to say:

> There are two of us in the family: me and my mother, leading a poor life. Everyday I have to beg in the streets for money, to support my mother. One day I was by the door of Mr. Liu's residence, and no one was around except the dog. I thought: If I hit the dog and make it bark, Mr. Liu would surely come out, and then I can beg money from him. I fetched a piece of brick, but instead of hitting the dog, I broke the commode by the door. Mrs. Liu appeared. She called me all sorts of names and cussed me out ten thousand times before I could even explain. And she called for Mr. Liu, who said: "A rich man like me loses only a few coppers if he beats a pauper like you to death." And I replied: "A pauper like me would not bother you with so much as a word when he meets you on high street, but if he sees you in the back alley, he'll kill you!" Mr. Liu didn't say anything, but his wife grabbed me and demanded a warranty of life, saying that I would be responsible for Mr. Liu's headache, fever, or even scratch on the small finger; and beyond one hundred days, it is none of my responsibility. . . .

(YCH, p. 678; emphasis mine)

The general outline of Wang's version concurs with what transpired on the stage as well as with the previous recitals of Mrs. Liu; but there are also important additions (underlined) to the earlier versions. First, by way of introduction, Wang slyly stresses his filial piety: it is for his mother that he begs in the streets. Second, he exaggerates the facts and paints Mrs. Liu blacker (as far as this incident is concerned, at least) than she is; on the other hand, he does not mention his unsuccessful attempt to charge Mr. Liu's dog with "biting" him. What is more important is that, perhaps inadvertently, Wang reminds the second judge that it was Mrs. Liu who wanted the warranty so badly. The suspicion here planted in the judge's mind must have played a part in his determination, later on, that "the entire case rests on Mrs. Liu" (YCH, p. 681). These "little" changes enhance our understanding of Wang Hsiao-erh and, because they work in his favor, are a factor in the reversal of his fortune. Wang's recapitulation is therefore functional, as Mrs. Liu's, in both instances, are not.

Another case of artistically questionable repetition involves a comic interlude in the prison. Soon after Wang is jailed for the alleged murder, a farmer played by the <u>ch'ou</u> 丑 (clown role)[35] appears:

> Farmer: I come to town everyday to sell straw. Those people in the tall building over there took two large baskets of straw on credit and just won't pay up. My mom accuses me of squandering the money on food. I'll try to collect the bill again today. (<u>He walks.</u>) Here we are. What?--the door locked so tightly in broad daylight? (<u>He knocks at the door.</u>) Open the door, Uncle!

> Jailor (<u>startled from his nap</u>): Ya! it must be the Clerk.-- Now wait a second: He would have pulled the string and rung the bell, and certainly would not bang at the door. (<u>He opens the door.</u>)

> Farmer: Uncle, pay me for the straw.

> Jailor (<u>grins</u>): Believe me, I've been looking for you too. Plait me a mat and I'll pay you for the straw. (Aside.) I'll trick him into the cell. (<u>Grabs the farmer's carrying pole and runs into the cell.</u>)

> Farmer: Give it back to me! (<u>Jailor pushes him into the cell.</u>) Uncle, why is it so dark in here? (<u>Jailor opens the skylight.</u>) And why is it that you grow human heads on these boards? Don't they bite? Bring the straw and I'll make a mat for you. (<u>He starts making thatch. Enter Clerk Chao.</u>)

> Chao: Here I am at the jail. I'll pull the bell rope.

> Jailor: Now it's the Clerk all right. What am I going to do with this one here? (<u>He puts a cangue on Farmer. Farmer looks frightened.</u>) Keep your mouth shut! If you say a single word, I'll beat you dead. (<u>He opens the door.</u>)

> Chao: Now don't you dare take a prisoner's bribe and set him free.

Jailor: I <u>dare</u> not, sir.

Chao: Bring Wang Hsiao-erh here. His case isn't concluded yet. Now, where are the two pieces of loot--
the silk kerchief with sesame print and the ring of
alloyed silver?

Wang: Brother, I was forced to make a false confession.
I really don't have them.

Chao: No flogging, no confession. Jailor, beat him!

(<u>Jailor beats Wang.</u>)

Wang: I can't stand the beating--I'll confess! Yes, yes,
yes: I put them under the slate by the well in the
vegetable garden of Liu the Cripple's, outside of
Hsiao-lin township.

Chao: Who's on duty in the yamen today?

Jailor: I am.

Chao: Then I'd like to have the kerchief and the ring
from you today. Sign here.

Jailor: Yes sir.

Chao: I haven't checked these prisoners for some time.

Jailor: But, brother, that's not your job--it's Clerk Hu's.

Chao: Who's this here?

Jailor: A horse-stealer.

Chao: And this?

Jailor: A clothes-stealer.

Chao (<u>pointing to Farmer</u>): And this?

Jailor: A ruffian stealer.

Chao: Good. He's the one I'd like to beat. (<u>He beats
Farmer.</u>) I'll beat you so you can remember me
well, you ruffian stealer! (<u>Exit.</u>)

Jailor (<u>releasing Farmer</u>): You may go now. Come
again tomorrow for your money.

Farmer: Yeah, I will--to look for your mother's stud.
Forget about the bill! (<u>Exit.</u>)

(<u>YCH</u>, pp. 672-73)

The episode is pregnant with meanings. On the more abstract level, it may be perceived as a miniature world of the injustice system in operation. The victimized prisoner is not given any chance; the shrewd jailor sees that everything works to his favor; and the unimaginative clerk is determined to conclude a case at all costs. To an outsider--in the person of the farmer--it is an incomprehensible, utterly impenetrable world. Even without giving it a stitch of allegorical clothing, however, the intrelude may still be appreciated as superb comedy. Thanks to the playwright's masterful use of language, light humor is blended with boisterous hilarity. As a result of the ludicrous incongruity involved, even the floggings seem devoid of their customary overtone of seriousness or pathos. In one case, the slyness of the jailor contrasts with the naiveté of the farmer. In the other, the clerk in a mad rush accepts so obvious a fabrication from the defendant with such complacency and earnestness that one finds a blurred line between the victimizer and the victim. Even more immediately attractive than either the allegorical or comical import, perhaps, was the appeal of the acrobatics and slapstick that are an implicit part and parcel of the prison scene; but they lie outside the domain of the present study.

The adroitly maneuvered episode must have pleased the playwright himself tremendously, for he has it retold twice by the farmer. Both recapitulations may be called "useful" in terms of the development of the drama, yet the two great virtues of the scene--the subtlety and vitality that result from characters interacting with one another in a farcically complex situation--are all lost in the straightforward narrations. In the first repeat, the farmer bumps into the monk--Mrs. Liu's lover--and unknowingly transmits the information about the supposed location of the kerchief and ring, thus facilitating the murderer's framing of Wang Hsiao-erh. The scene takes place as follows:

Monk: Good brother, whence did you come?

Farmer: People in the tall house over there owe me
money for two baskets of straw, and just wouldn't
pay up. My mom suspects I squandered the money
on food, so I went again today to collect it. The
door was bolted in broad daylight, and I had to hol-
ler. Inside, I couldn't see anyone. "Brother,"
says I. "Why is it so dark in here?" So he pushed
something overhead and there was light! He has a
floor full of boards from which human heads grow.
He asked me to thatch a mat, and while I was at it,
someone came to the door and he became frightened.

He took a piece of board--it had a hole in it--and put
it round my neck. He pushed me onto the floor and told
me not to say a word. Then, see here, someone en-
tered with two wings on his head. "Bring Wang Hsiao-
erh here," he says. He demanded from Wang the silk
kerchief with sesame print and the ring of alloyed
silver. Wang said, "I don't have them." And, good
heavens! he kept beating Wang until Wang was soaked
with blood through and through. At last Wang said,
"Yes, yes, yes! I put them under the slate by the well
in the vegetable garden of Liu the Cripple's, outside
of Hsiao-lin township. . . .

(Monk, having listened attentively, exits.)

And the one in the hat with wings makes his rounds
and turned to me. "Who's this?" he asked. And that
guy made up a name and called me "a ruffian stealer."
Now, brother, you're a smart fellow, but have you
ever heard of such a thing as a thief who stole ruffians?

(He looks back to see.)

Ya! The damned rascal is gone! Or did I just see a
ghost?--and I kept talking to him! I'd better go now.
(Exit.)

(YCH, p. 673)

The farmer's monologue takes place almost immediately after he is
released from the jail, and it supplies practically no information that
was not presented in the prison scene. Nevertheless, one can see that
to have the clownish farmer go on babbling and complaining after the
monk had taken his secretive leave is good theater.

In contrast, the second recapitulation is a disaster. This time he
recalls the incident as he faces the judge of the second trial:

Farmer: The other day I came for the straw-money. He
took me into the jail and asked me to thatch a mat. As
I was doing it, someone came to the door. This fellow,
frightened, took a piece of board which had a hole in it,
placed it round my neck, and pushed me onto the floor.
He told me not to say a word. Then a man enters, with

two wings on his head. No sooner had he sat down
than he called for Wang Hsiao-erh. I forgot what he
said, but he kept beating Wang, until Wang was soaked
with blood through and through. And Wang said, "Yes,
yes, yes!--just stop beating! The silk kerchief with
sesame print and the ring of alloyed silver were placed
under the slate by the well in the vegetable garden of
Liu the Cripple's, outside of Hsiao-lin township."
The man then said, "I haven't checked these prisoners
for a long time." He asked the jailor what kind of
thieves they were, and the jailor explained that they
were horse-stealers and clothes-stealers. Then he
came to me, asked, "What's this one?" And that son
of a bitch made up a name out of nowhere and called me
"a ruffian stealer." You are a smart fellow, Uncle, but
tell me, would you like to be a thief that steals ruffians?
At last he set me free. Someone appeared from I don't
know where and bumped into me, his hat bumped off his
head. And I saw he was a Taoist monk. . . .

Jailor: Come to think of it, I also saw a Taoist monk on my
way to fetch the kerchief and ring.

Judge: Did the monk ask you anything, my son?

Farmer: Yes indeed. And I told him about the Wang Hsiao-
erh story. And all of a sudden he vanished--just like
that. . . .

(YCH, pp. 680-81)

The crucial point here is the farmer's mention of the Taoist monk,
which serves as a reminder to the jailor. The bulk of his lengthy recital,
however, is tedious, being totally unwarranted and strikingly less artistically manipulated than the previous recapitulation. It is also important
to notice that, at this point, the third occasion for a retelling arises,
but the playwright spares his audience another bombardment by simply
having the farmer say, "And I told him about the Wang Hsiao-erh story."
Obviously he could have by-passed the undesirable second repetition as
well, but he didn't. His shift to summary at last has come too late; he
has gone over the same material one time too many.

The Child Shen-nu-erh

Taken as a whole, language in The Child Shen-nu-erh (anon.) is handled with uneven craft. On the prose and verse levels, there are undesirable repetitions and verbal play, but also effective jokes. On the lyrical level, it is unique--at least among the judgment reversal plays--in that the singing role changes hands more than once: the cheng-mo 正末 (male lead) is given to Li Te-jen, the old servant, and Judge Pao in that order. The arrangement, stemming presumably from internal dramatic considerations (Li and the servant have to relinquish their roles in time because of death), has certain advantages. Instead of the usual one or two, three characters in this play are allowed the use of arias, a vehicle proven to be effective for the expression of deeper and subtler feelings. There is also an appearance of variety, even though it is most likely that one and the same actor, the star, did all the singing roles. On the other hand, this arrangement poses some problems as well. For instance, it makes the development of consistent poetic imagery and the portrayal of characters a more difficult task, particularly in the cases of Li Te-jen and Judge Pao, each of whom enjoys too short a stint on stage--one act, to be precise. But let me outline the action first.

At the insistence of La-mei, his wife, the henpecked Li Te-yi proposes that he and his brother, Te-jen, cease living under the same roof--each taking his own share of the family estate. Te-jen's traditional way of thinking abhors such aberration, and he is forced into accepting the alternative--that he divorce his wife. Even before he can sign the bill of divorcement, however, shame and shock claim his life; surviving him are his wife, A-Ch'en,[36] and their only child, Shen-nu-erh. The greedy La-mei, eyeing the other half of the fortune, strangles Shen-nu-erh whom her husband has brought home. Shen-nu-erh appears in a dream to his former servant, the elderly yüan-kung 院公 (factotum) to tell the gruesome story. A search by A-Ch'en and the servant ensues. But, instead of bringing the murderer to light, A-Ch'en herself is charged with the deed and sentenced to death. In the end the ghost of Shen-nu-erh manifests itself to Judge Pao, and justice is restored.

The murder of Shen-nu-erh is committed early in the second act (YCH, p. 563); in the same act, the deed is recapitulated three times. The first one takes place when, after the initial search for the missing child has failed, the fatigued servant falls asleep by the door, still waiting for his young master:

(The ghost of Child appears.)

Ghost: I am Shen-nu-erh. The old servant took me to play
in the street. I wanted a puppet, and he went to buy it
for me. I was waiting by the bridge when I chanced to
see my uncle. He took me to his house, where my aunt
strangled me. I was buried in the ditch and covered with
a slate. I doubt dear old yüan-kung knows about all this,
so I'll appear in his dream. Here we are. Dear yüan-
kung, open the door!

Servant: Ai-yo! The young master is home! Come in,
master. . . .

(YCH, p. 565)

And seeing that his entreating is to no avail, the old servant asks the
tearful Shen-nu-erh: "Dear master, did someone bully you?" The
enquiry gives rise to a second recital as the ghost replies,

Dear old yüan-kung, when you left to buy the puppet, I stayed
on the bridge and waited for you. Then I happened to see my
uncle, who took me to his home. My aunt strangled me with
a rope, and buried me in the ditch, covering me with a slate.
Dear yüan-kung, do something!

(YCH, p. 565)

The servant, startled from his dream, immediately reports to his mis-
tress--and for the third time the audience is obliged to listen to what is
basically the same, though duller, story:

Very tired, I fell asleep by the door and dreamed of master
Shen-nu-erh. He said his uncle took him home and the aunt
strangled him. Now, he was buried in the ditch, covered
with a slate. . . .

(YCH, pp. 565-66)

Needless to say, having a ghost appear on the stage and give its
own account of the gruesome tale can produce tremendous theatrical
effects, and a playwright may find the temptation to do so too great to
resist. In this case, however, while the second recapitulation may
possibly be justified on both theatrical and dramatic grounds, the first
one appears unnecessary and the third one considerably lacking in art.
One must assume that the audience, having witnessed the aunt murder

her nephew in cold blood, has perhaps even less appetite for several lackluster "prosaic" repetitions in swift succession. As a matter of fact, the playwright himself might have felt the same way, for there seems to have been a conscious, deliberate effort on his part to avoid too much redundancy: in the repeating process, the story gets thinner and thinner. Be that as it may, the repetition has nevertheless placed too great an emphasis on the revelation of the dream--as if it were the turning point of the entire play. But is it?

For quite some time in the third act, the audience is led to believe so. Pursuing the lead provided by the ghost of Shen-nu-erh, the grieved mother and her servant hurry to Li Te-yi's place:

Servant: Open up, open up!

Te-yi (frightened): Woman, they're here! What shall we do? (Opening the door.) I'll answer the door.

Servant (grabs him): You wanted all the inheritance so much that you strangled the child. You're not going to get away with it!

Te-yi (aside): What'll be the end of this? How am I to cover it up?

La-mei: Auntie, what brings you here?

A-Ch'en: I am here to look for Shen-nu-erh. He said his uncle brought him to his house.

La-mei: Why would I see your Shen-nu-erh? Why should he come to my house?

Servant: Shen-nu-erh is in your house!

Te-yi: You old clown! Why would Shen-nu-erh come here?

A-Ch'en: Because his uncle took him home.

Te-yi: I didn't! Let's go and ask the neighbors--and see if anyone can prove otherwise!

Servant (sings):　　　　　　紅繡鞋 Hung hsiu-hsieh

It's no use resisting. Nor is there need
To rouse the neighbors for Shen-nu-erh's corpse.
For it is hidden in this ditch. . . .

La-mei (frightened): Who told you it was buried in the ditch? Where is it? Where is it?

Servant (<u>sings</u>):

> Child,
> As I follow the clue of the dream,
> She suddenly begins to panic and
> Falters at every word. Why?
> --"The thief knows no peace of mind."

Te-yi: Did I? Who can prove it? You go ahead and find him if you can.

Servant: Keep quiet. I'll find him all right.

> (<u>He sings.</u>)   迎仙客   <u>Ying hsien-k'o</u>

> There has been no rain,
> But why is here so muddy, wet?

La-mei: It's just the damned water we spilt.

Servant (<u>sings</u>):

> You claim it's just water, but
> Who added dirt to it?

La-mei: There was a hollow there, so we put some hay and dirt on it, and poured some water. --But this is <u>our</u> business: mind your own!

Servant (<u>sings</u>):

> Why is the slate out of its place?

La-mei: "Dig ditches while the sun shines, and you won't have mud when it rains." And so I dug the ditch, yes I did.

Servant (<u>sings</u>):

> And what is blocking the ditch?

La-mei: The rain was heavy, and naturally the water overflowed. --Where is Shen-nu-erh? Go and seek him out.

Servant (<u>sings</u>):

> Don't you rush me;
> I intend to take time and seek him out.

> (<u>says</u>)

> Mistress, they hid the corpse.

>La-mei: Come over here, husband. This woman is young
>and cannot stand an empty chamber; she has a secret
>lover. They murdered the child. . . .

(<u>YCH</u>, p. 567)

In all fairness, it must be conceded that the above is for the most
part a good piece of suspense, showing some knowledge of the psychology
of guilt. Unfortunately, however, the search is abandoned just when its
successful completion is in sight. In an arbitrary turn of events, the
offense and defense abruptly change places, and A-Ch'en now faces the
charge of murdering the child with the assistance of her lover, whoever
he is supposed to be. Murder will out; but not yet. It may be argued
that to have the <u>yüan-kung</u> discover the corpse would mean the end of
the drama. True, but to have the clue underscored with three straight
recapitulations and then dropped in such a careless and hurried manner
seems to me a clumsy way of lengthening the piece.

Immediately after the abortive search, the scene shifts to the first
trial in the courthouse, where we are in for the conventional jokes aimed
at the incorrigible officials. Both the Prefect-Judge's entrance verse,

>The judge is clean as water,
>His clerk, white as flour;
>When the two are mixed together,
>You get a muddled picture.

(<u>YCH</u>, p. 568)

and the Clerk's,

>Though not smart about laws and rules,
>I'm naturally able and clean.
>Though fear of a supervisor coming to check
>Causes disorder in my spleen.

(<u>YCH</u>, p. 568)

are strongly reminiscent of the self-ridicule by Clerk Hsiao and his
incompetent boss in <u>The Mo-ho-lo Doll</u> (above, p. 39ff.). Even the
trick for extorting bribes is identical:

Clerk Sung (<u>taking a close look [at Li-Te-yi]</u>):

Well, this fellow--haven't I seen him before? Oh yes,
oh yes. The other day, while patrolling, I stopped by
his door and asked for a seat, but he refused to oblige
me. My boy, now you've made your way to this yamen
of mine! Chang Ch'ien, drag him over here.

Steward: Yes, sir.

(Li Te-yi handing over silver and sticking out some
fingers.)

Clerk Sung (looking carefully): What's wrong with those
other two fingers of yours--rotted? Now you cut that
out and deliver [the money] this evening. . . .

(YCH, p. 568)

There are, of course, a couple of minor differences. For instance, the risible explanation of the Clerk's official title (ling-shih
令史) is not present in Doll. And, whereas in Doll the judge kneels
before the plaintiff because "whoever comes to the court and makes
complaint is my daily bread for which I have great respect," in Child
the judge kneels before his clerk because "there is a murder case which
is beyond me and for which I need your help" (YCH, p. 568). Basically,
however, the verbal play in this comic scene is the same in both dramas.
The question of whether Meng Han-ch'ing's Doll precedes the anonymous
author's Child or vice versa need not concern us here; tsa-chü being
the highly stylized and conventionalized theater that it is, there is perhaps never much to be gained from inquiries into who "originates" what.
Instead, it seems to me more sensible and fruitful to pay attention to
how well the convention is manipulated to effect dramatic purposes. In
this respect, the jokes in Child, like their counterparts in Doll, make
their point; not only do they provide comic relief after the merciless
murder and the suspenseful search for the corpse, but they also fore-
warn the audience of what to expect in the trial.

In contrast to these puns, however, the merit of another jeu de
mots in the second trial is doubtful. There, Judge Pao detects something fishy about the case, but he lacks evidence to prove the original
verdict wrong. He wonders aloud (YCH, p. 573): "If I could get a witness (kan-cheng 干證)--how nice that would be (k'o-yeh hao-yeh 可也
好也)!" Whereupon a court steward named Ho Cheng 何正 steps
forward, thinking that the judge has just called him (his name is supposed to pun with k'o and cheng). It is as if the judge, by saying "I
would like to have a witness," has conjured up a witness by the name of

Witwould. Surely Judge Pao needs Ho Cheng to reverse the verdict,
but the audience deserves something better than this unconvincingly
strained wordplay--even given the casual, almost accidental, fashion
in which justice is usually restored in most of the courtroom plays. The
disappointment is further compounded when one contrasts the feeble pun
with the vividness of the scene in which Ho Cheng witnessed Li Te-yi
carrying Shen-nu-erh away with him ("wedge," YCH, p. 562).

Finally, a passing remark on the lyrics in this play. I have suggested that, because they are shared by three characters, it is difficult
for the lyrics to form consistent poetic imagery or present compelling
portraits of character. An illustration of this problem is found in the
opening lines of Li Te-jen, in the first act:

点绛唇 Tien chiang-ch'un

An honest fellow since childhood,
I have never been good at economy:
So long as nothing disturbs me,
I care nothing for the value of gold.

混江龍 Hun-chiang lung

Consider this life of man.
The rich people nowadays are no longer fools.
Though yesterday you might be rosy-cheeked,
Today your head and back may be bending.
As the sunshine outside the window hurries away,
So the shadows of the table flowers travel across
      the seats. . . .

(YCH, p. 557)

Even in the present ambiguous state, the passage contains the carpe
diem theme, probably resulting from a sense of contentment or even
complacency. The speaker's untimely death in the hands of his brother
and sister-in-law whose appetite for material gain is insatiable may,
therefore, be meant for irony. But since Li Te-jen has to forsake the
stage even before the first act ends, the theme remains where it is,
and the irony is not further realized.

Only the elderly yüan-kung, who sings arias in the "wedge" and
the second and third acts, is given opportunity to develop his moral
outrage in the face of evil and corruption. In the corpse-hunting scene
we have already seen him shouting "Keep quiet!" to the murderers.

When he and his mistress are on their way to the house of Te-yi, after
the truth of the murder has been revealed to him by the ghost, the servant sings:

粉蝶兒 Fen-tieh-erh

They breach morality,
And would not let us live.
That knave has a hundred plots and schemes;
His slanderous wife is also a murderer.
Can I be forgiving?--Certainly not with <u>them</u>!
I am going to hail them to the high court--even if
I have to drag them there by their clothes.

醉春風 Tsui ch'un-feng

They are my deadly enemies:
Never could we reconcile . . . .
. . . .
Though they be gifted with the persuasion of Su Ch'in
Or the rhetoric of Lu Ku,
I doubt [they] could defend [themselves].

(<u>YCH</u>, p. 566)

With the same indignation, the servant rushes to the defense of his mistress when the latter is harrassed and bullied by corrupt officials. Here
is an example:

Clerk Sung: If she has an adulterous lover, give me his
name quick!

Servant (<u>sings</u>):

<u>Ya</u>! For an honest wife she is, whom
You accuse, without evidence, of adultery.
<u>Ai</u>! You are a "murky tower"*--
An impenetrable, stupid official!
Intent on extracting the deposition,
You have no respect for facts.

---

* The Chinese phrase here is 水晶塔, literally meaning "crystal
pagoda," with a distinct implication of 浮圖透頂 (or "a pagoda that
is extremely clear"), which then puns on 胡塗透頂 (or "extremely
muddle-headed"). Cf. Wang Chi-ssu (III), 15.

Clerk Sung: Confess!

Servant (<u>sings</u>):

> "Go ahead and confess," you say.
> But, sir, consider this:
> Did she do it or didn't she?

(<u>YCH</u>, p. 570)

Only rarely do we see in courtroom <u>tsa-chü</u> a defendant adhere to his conviction, unswayed by the threat of the judges. It is particularly striking in this case, because the low social status of the speaker makes him the natural prey of unscrupulous officialdom.

III. THE MANIPULATION OF CHARACTERS

Conventionality Versus Individuality

It has often been remarked that the characters in Yüan drama are
types rather than individuals. This is an observation that is suggested
by both the role classification system of the Yüan dynasty theater and
the nomenclature of dramatis personae used in extant texts. The former
distinguishes players according to such set roles as "leading man,"
"leading woman," "old man," "old woman," "child," and so on. The
latter almost always gives to servants such conventional appellations
as Chang Ch'ien 張千 (in the case of a male) or Mei-hsiang 梅香 (in
the case of a female), while addressing persons of higher status by their
formal or official titles--"Prefect," "Chief Clerk," "Lord," and so on.
There is little effort, it appears, to individualize dramatic characters.

The causes behind such a phenomenon have been the subject of
speculation by scholars in recent years. Professor Chung-wen Shih,
for instance, attributes it to the literary, ethical, and "theatrical"
traditions of old China.[1] By literary tradition she means the character
portrayals in pre-Yüan prose writing (particularly Ssu-ma Ch'ien's
Shih-chi 史記 or Historical Records), which provides Yüan playwrights
with literary models emphasizing the typical. Her "ethical tradition"
refers to the doctrine that stresses propriety, extolling the fulfillment
of one's proper function in the universe over individuation or self-
consciousness. And the theatrical tradition is the role system mentioned
above. Henry W. Wells, who also finds that "the Chinese theatre in
particular cherished the notion of types," approaches the issue by locating
and establishing the influences of mythology and history.[2] He seems to
suggest a correlation between the lack of "human" gods in China (as
opposed to the humanized deities on the Olympus) and the Chinese playwright's lack of interest in individualized character portrayal. But he
is quick to modify his theory by observing that those characters who are
also historical personages--and there are many of them in classical
Chinese theater--bring "a special conviction of personality" to the stage

85

because they bear historical names and perform actions which "the audiences at least credited as historical."[3]

However fascinating, useful, and important to the elucidation of the Chinese mind, the issue of types vs. individuals properly concerns historians and not critics of Chinese drama and, fortunately, need not detain us here. Suffice it to note, at the outset, that the characters peopling the Yüan stage are conceived of in Theophrastian rather than naturalistic terms. There is no need to be apologetic about it either, for the function of a character in any play rests first and foremost in his contribution to the drama as a whole. As J. L. Styan puts it, "[a character] discharges his meaning in the context of a scene."[4] What this implies, of course, is that to the extent a character fits in the design of the play and effects the desired dramatic purpose, he should be judged a success or a failure. The question of whether the actions he performs are "well-motivated" does not necessarily enter. In this connection it is well to recall Madeleine Doran's judicious words:

> Perhaps we are more troubled by what seems the failure of
> repetitive form in many Elizabethan dramatic characters
> because we have been rendered too sophisticated in our ex-
> pectation by the characters in modern fiction. Moreover,
> in reading Elizabethan plays instead of seeing them we are
> the more easily led to judge them by a set of standards
> foreign to them.[5]

Substitute Yüan for Elizabethan in the passage, and the validity of its caution still holds.

Besides, type characters offer certain advantages in both the creative and the re-creative processes of the drama. On one hand, they enable the playwright to present, with considerable ease, his dramatis personae in a consistent and coherent fashion; on the other, the preconditioned audience may readily supply for itself what these type characters represent.[6] One of the results is that the playwright can then concentrate more on other areas of the drama, such as--in the case of Yüan tsa-chü--poetry, singing, dancing, the plot, the miming, and the acrobatics--all of which are essential to the total the-atrical experience and fulfill expectations of the spectator.

To recognize certain advantages of type characters, however, is not to reduce the value of character analysis; much less should it serve as an excuse for critics to relinquish what may prove an illuminating as well as intriguing area of dramatic criticism. One distinguishes even among the most trite stock characters fine shades of dissimilarities in personality, mannerism, and outlook. But character analysis, however fascinating it may be, should not be carried out as an end in itself; it is most rewarding when conducted with a view to the character's various functions in and contributions to the play. In what way, for instance, does he advance the progress of the play? How does he enlarge the vision or enhance the significance of the drama? What difference does his presence on stage make with respect to the dramatic impact? In short: how does a character help shape a play? Attempts to answer these questions can lead us to a more sophisticated understanding of the drama.

With Yüan tsa-chü, the task of character analysis is twofold: some characters are strictly conventional while others appear to be more the products of the playwright's invention. In the following pages, I shall address myself to both kinds as they are found in the judgment reversal plays. The first section, dealing with the conventional, examines the major stock characters: the villain, the victim, and the judge. The major topics discussed are: the interrelationships among characters of these three categories most frequently encountered in our select group, their general features, and their dramatic functions. Also considered in this section is the practice of a single singing role and its implication for the balance or imbalance of cast.

The second section will dwell on the less glamorous characters-- characters who are not singing roles or even familiar faces, whose time on stage is brief, yet who contribute significantly to the drama in their various small ways. Although seldom in the limelight, they are often the ones that spark and animate the play; exactly how this is achieved will be the subject explored. If in the stock characters and leading roles we perceive the Yüan playwright conforming to convention, we also discern in the "minor" characters his striving for invention. Both the treatment of convention and the handling of invention are crucial to the success of his drama, but it is against this effort to transcend the barrier of convention that his creative vitality as playwright should be measured.

Indispensable in every judgment reversal play are of course the villain, the victim, and the two kinds of officials, the good and the bad. As a rule, the villain dominates the play from the beginning to at least the second trial, when he is upstaged by the righteous judge. Till then he is the prime mover, so to speak. The victim, on the contrary, is usually passive and pathetic; whereas the villain acts, the victim is merely acted upon, sometimes even without reacting in turn. The latter's situation is further jeopardized when the villain is joined by a judge corrupt or inept (or, more likely, both); it is only with the arrival of the more scrupulous official that the victim is finally rescued from triumphant iniquity. Surprisingly enough, though, the good judge and the bad one have so much in common that it would be difficult to tell one from the other were it not for the professed moral sense of one and the professed lack of it in the other.

The villain

In six of the seven judgment reversal plays, the actual crime is murder. (In the exception, Rescue of the Filial Son, the alleged murder never took place.) But there is more to the villainy. The murderer not only does the foul deed, he also cleverly shifts blame for it to someone else: a close kin of the deceased or a total stranger is usually the scapegoat. The false accusation, its potential threat as well as actual damage to the victim, and its successful resolution--these, more than the murder per se, form the nucleus around which the dramatic interest is built.

Like most characters in Yüan tsa-chü, the villain speaks his mind freely and openly. There are several ways by which he can take the audience into his confidence: he may discuss his seamy plot with his accomplice, deliver a monologue, or address the audience directly in a soliloquy. Take, for example, The Chalk Circle, where all three methods are employed in Act I. Here the arch-villainess is Mrs. Ma, who, after reciting a doggerel entrance piece (q.v. pp. 63-4, above), addresses the audience in a typical, brazen manner:

> I'm Lord Ma's legal wife.--He has a concubine, by the
> name of, er, Hai-t'ang, I believe. They have a child,
> now five years old.--And there's my Clerk Chao, a jolly
> handsome fellow; and he has a line of goods as long as a
> donkey's! We have an amorous relationship. My simple
> wish is to undo my husband, so that Clerk Chao and I may
> be husband and wife forever. Since my lord is not home
> today, I've called for Clerk Chao. He should be here any
> minute now.

(YCH, pp. 1108-9)

When Clerk Chao joins Mrs. Ma on stage, the following dialogue ensues:

> Chao: Ma'am, what do you want me for?
>
> Mrs. Ma: I summoned you for just one thing. The two of us have been going along stealthily, but when is this secrecy going to end? I'm determined to get a dose of poison and murder Lord Ma. We two can then be husband and wife forever. How wonderful that would be!
>
> Chao: You're not just some harlot that I chanced to meet! I adore you as I would my mother! If this be in your mind, can it not be shared by me as well?--I have had the poison ready for quite some time now! (He reaches for the poison and hands it to Mrs. Ma.) Here it is. I'll leave it with you, for I have to go to the yamen. (Exit.)
>
> Mrs. Ma: Clerk Chao is gone. I'll put the poison away and bide my time. . . .
>
> (YCH, p. 1109)

Neither Mrs. Ma nor Clerk Chao has made any attempt to conceal the naked truth. Euphemism would be out of place.

If that is the case with soliloquy and dialogue, one knows what to expect from monologue. Later in the same act, after Mrs. Ma has fulfilled her first wish by successfully poisoning her husband, she starts to brood over her next move, which is how to claim Hai-t'ang's child. Alone on stage, she thinks aloud:

> See? She's trapped by my scheme! The entire family fortune, along with the child, will soon be mine.
>
> (She reconsiders.)
>
> Ha! You'd better think it over: the child is not mine by birth. She'd call as witnesses the two grannies who delivered the baby and shaved its head, as well as the neighbors who have watched him grow up. If they do not testify to my advantage at the court, all my effort will go for naught.
>
> Now, the black pupils in human eyes cannot resist the lure of white silver. I'll simply have to take care of that. To each and every one of them I'll offer one tael of silver, and

they'll stand by me. If only Clerk Chao were here so I
could talk it over with him. . . .

(YCH, p. 1115)

The monologue begins with complacency over her recent victory, but
develops consequences and action to come. As in the previous two
instances, the why and how of a nefarious scheme are detailed for the
audience.

Not all revelations are done thus. They may assume a simpler,
less elaborate form, especially when other hints are available to make
certain the audience understands exactly what the villain means. A
case in point is the following speech by Li Wen-tao in the second act of
The Mo-ho-lo Doll. (Wen-tao has just learned from Kao Shan, the well-
meaning but unsuspecting peddler, that his cousin Li Te-ch'ang lies ill
in the Temple of Five Way General, "with a purse a hundred times its
former weight" [YCH, p. 1372].)

As the saying goes, "Man proposes, Heaven complies."
So he's taken ill now. I'll not tell my sister-in-law but go
straight to the outskirts of the town [where the temple is]
and kill him with this dose of poison. His wife will then be
mine, as will his money and properties. . . .

(YCH, p. 1372)

Isolated from the context as it is, only a murky picture of the triangular
relationship among Wen-tao, his cousin, and his sister-in-law emerges
from this quote. The proverb, in particular, appears utterly irrelevant
and unwarranted.

In fact, however, the audience has known from the start that Wen-
tao lusts after his sister-in-law. He has already propositioned Yü-
niang: in the opening scene of the play, the audience is allowed to guess
the less-than-noble intentions Wen-tao harbors toward his sister-in-
law:

[Li Te-ch'ang is leaving home.]

Yü-niang: Husband, since you're leaving today on your
business trip, would you mind if I tell you something?

Te-ch'ang: What is it?

Yü-niang: Your cousin has time and again attempted to
flirt with me--

Te-ch'ang: Silence! Why didn't you tell me sooner? Why
did you wait until the moment I leave? Wife: don't
you ever bring that up again--just take good care of
the household and be mindful. . . .

(YCH, p. 1386)

The audience knows of course that Te-ch'ang cannot have been entirely
unaware of the situation; as a matter of fact, it appears that he himself
immediately contradicts his feigned ignorance as he goes on to sing
(Shang-hua-shih 賞花時): "You and my cousin have always been at
odds/[to the audience] That's why I admonished her as I did" (YCH,
p. 1368). The impropriety of Wen-tao's behavior is also suggested by
his own father, who gives him this most thinly veiled warning:

Old Li: Li Wen-tao: now that your cousin has gone on
business, you must not go to your sister-in-law's
place except for a very good reason. Otherwise,
I won't let you get away with it! . . .

(YCH, p. 1368)

In addition to indirect allusions to Wen-tao's unsavory nature, we
have as well the saucy knave's own testimony to his impure intentions.
Listen to him talk at the beginning of Act I:

Wen-tao: My cousin, Li Te-ch'ang, is gone on a business
trip, leaving my sister-in-law at home, alone. I'm
madly in love with her, but my father admonished me
to avoid her house.

Well, now, I'll call this a visit--I'll conceal it
from my father though--and see if I can make out.
Whether she submits or not, I have nothing to lose. . . .

(YCH, p. 1369)

Guessing Wen-tao's wicked intent, Yü-niang calls Old Li for help,
whose control over his lascivious son, however, seems formal rather
than real:

Yü-naing: Cousin Wen-tao came to my chamber and annoyed
me, and I wanted you to know.

Old Li (catches sight of Wen-tao): What are you doing here
again? (He beats Wen-tao. Exit Wen-tao.) If he ever
comes again, just call me. I'm not going to let him
get away with it! I'll go and give that good-for-nothing
some more of the same! (Exit.)

Yü-niang: When will this end? I'll close the store for
today. Li Te-ch'ang, when will you return? Oh, what
a miserable creature I am!

(YCH, p. 1369)

By Wen-tao's own account, we know that he is "madly in love" with his
sister-in-law and has no qualms whatsoever in taking advantage of his
cousin's absence. The dialogue between Yü-niang and Old Li further
reveals that this is not Wen-tao's first advance on his sister-in-law:
"Why are you here again?" and "When will this end?", for instance.
The repeated threat of Old Li ("I'm not going to let him get away with
it!"), on the other hand, simply betrays his inability to curb the mis-
conduct of his unprincipled son. With these notions in mind, the audience can be counted on to appreciate Wen-tao's more obscure monologue
in the second act, quoted above. In other words, whether the revelation
comes in the form of soliloquy, dialogue, or monologue and whether it
is detailed or sketchy, the audience is always kept abreast of the
villain's intentions.

The second convention associated with the villain underscores his
complete impudence and relentless wickedness. Once the unspeakable
deed is accomplished, the murderer immediately places the blame on
the scapegoat of his choice. He then proceeds to offer the selected victim, ostensibly as a gesture of magnanimity, two alternatives: the
victim has a choice between private and official settlements. By defini-
tion, private settlement means to follow the dictates of the villain and
be coerced; the villain stands to gain. Official settlement, on the other
hand, means physical torture beyond endurance for the victim; the villain has nothing to lose. To illustrate, here is a scene from Injustice
to Tou Ngo (the translation is based on Professor Shih's,[7] altered in
places to highlight the convention):

Donkey Chang: Fine! You have poisoned my father; yet
you expect to get out of it scatheless!

Granny Ts'ai: Child, how is this going to end?

Tou Ngo: What poison would I have? When he was asking for salt and vinegar, he put the poison in the soup himself.

(sings) 隔尾 Ke-wei

This fellow tricked my old mother into keeping you.
You yourself have poisoned your father.
Whom do you think you can frighten?

Donkey Chang: My own father--to say that I, his own son, poisoned him, nobody would believe it. (Shouts) Neighbors, neighbors, listen! Tou Ngo has poisoned my father!

Granny Ts'ai: Stop! Don't get so worked up. You scare me to death.

Donkey Chang: Are you afraid, then?

Granny Ts'ai: Indeed I am afraid.

Donkey Chang: You want to be let off, then?

Granny Ts'ai: Indeed I do.

Donkey Chang: Then tell Tou Ngo to give me what I want, to call me dear, beloved husband three times, and I'll let you off.

Granny Ts'ai: Child, you had better give in now.

Tou Ngo: Mother, how can you say such a thing? . . .

Donkey Chang: Tou Ngo, you have poisoned my father.
Do you want to settle the matter officially or privately?

Tou Ngo: What do you mean by officially or privately?

Donkey Chang: If you want to settle the matter officially, I shall take you to court, where you will be thoroughly interrogated. Frail as you are, you will not be able to stand the beating and will have to confess to the murder of my father. If you want to settle privately, you had better become my wife soon--and what a good bargain for you!

(YCH, pp. 1506-7)

Obviously, a psychological war has started, and Donkey Chang has the offensive; and now that Granny Ts'ai is prepared to surrender, he almost wins it too.

But the villain's neat formula never works out as smoothly as he would have it. Confident that his innocence will eventually be upheld and his name cleared, the victim, as a rule, refuses to compromise himself (not at this point at any rate). Instead, he spurns the suggestion of "private" settlement and would go straight to court. In Injustice, Tou Ngo's immediate and unflinching response to Donkey Chang's proposal is: "Since I did not poison your old father, I would rather go with you to see the magistrate!" (YCH, p. 1507) Since such a choice is really no choice, the convention of offering two alternatives must be regarded as just another means to heighten the devilish disposition of the murderer who also threatens and bullies, leaving no stone unturned where his own benefit is concerned. Villains in Yüan drama are nothing if not villainous.

The convention of "which poison would you like" appears in four of the seven judgment reversal plays; its absence in the other three may be explained in terms of motivation (or the lack of it). In The Gold Phoenix Hairpins, for instance, Tiger Li the murderer cleverly chooses to stay away from it all: for him, the less visibility the better. In Rescue of the Filial Son, the plaintiff is the victim Ch'un-hsiang's own mother and not a bully; while the mother's ability to judge may be a bit questionable, there can be little doubt that she acts solely and sincerely on behalf of her (supposedly) wronged daughter. And in Judgment on the Kerchief, Mrs. Liu takes Wang Hsiao-erh to court out of necessity: she has to make a spectacle of her "indignation" over the death of her husband and protect her lover, coauthor and executioner of her plot. In these cases, either a private settlement is impossible to arrange or there is nothing to be gained from it as far as the miscreant's personal interest goes. In the four plays where the convention is utilized, however, such an arrangement in private, if agreed to by the victim, would mean total victory for the unconscionable schemer. He would then be entitled to the legacy of the murdered (as in The Chalk Circle and The Child Shen-nu-erh) or succeed in marrying the woman-victim against her will (Injustice to Tou Ngo) or both (The Mo-ho-lo Doll).

There may be another, more practical, explanation for the absence of the "choice" convention. Note that in Hairpins, Rescue, and Kerchief, the corpses are found in public places, with the murderers nowhere to be had. The publicity given to these cases of homicide leaves the survivors virtually no alternative other than to bring their cases to court:

to do otherwise would be inconceivable or incriminatory. However, the circumstances surrounding the deaths in the other plays are different. The deceased is in each case a member of the plaintiff's household (also the defendant's, except in Child). Shen-nu-erh's corpse (Child) is successfully concealed in the ditch and the other three deaths, brought about by poison, can be disguised for a while as natural. It is at least theoretically feasible for the villains in these cases to attempt out-of-court settlements without inviting too much public attention or suspicion. Now, if this and the other explanation are not too far off the mark, an unwritten law governing the use of the convention can perhaps be deduced: villains are to be portrayed in the most unequivocal terms, provided that plausibility is not seriously violated.

A bold exposition of malicious intent and a "generous" gesture to compromise or reconcile, then, are two of the most common features in the presentation of villainous characters. It is also conventional for them to bribe venal officials and clerks responsible for the first trial, but this topic will be taken up in conjunction with the discussion below on the judges. Another feature to be observed in this connection is the role of villainess, which seems to be spectacular. This too will be given fuller consideration as we come to the individual character studies.

The victim

We have seen that it is a common practice for the wicked characters to offer their all-too-honest (not to say gullible) victims a "choice." We have also seen that it is equally customary for the victim to choose to go to court. He does it in the belief that at the end of the judicial process he will be vindicated and his good name restored. Tou Ngo's (Injustice) retort to Donkey Chang is, "Since I did not poison your old father, I'd rather go with you to see the magistrate"; and Li A-Ch'en (Child) rejects the murderers' blackmailing suggestion for a private settlement and declares, "With a clear conscience, I have nothing to fear: we shall see the officials." Yet these flashes of self-confidence do not last long. No matter how firmly resolved he may appear at the beginning of the long fight for his own cause, the victim invariably gives in to the harsh torture inflicted by insensate yamen officials. When Donkey Chang warns Tou Ngo that she may not be physically able to withstand the beating at court, he is not exaggerating the case.

As a convention, the change of mind--and of heart--in the victim is by and large taken for granted; usually nothing much is made of it.

For instance, here is Wang Hsiao-erh's confession in <u>Kerchief</u>:

> Mrs. Liu: In less than ten days after he signed the war-
> ranty of life, Wang Hsiao-erh killed my husband out-
> side the city. Be my advocate, good clerk!
>
> Wang: Have pity, good clerk! How dare I kill anybody?
>
> Clerk: You signed the warranty of life and in less than
> ten days Liu P'ing-yüan is killed. Who could've done
> it if you didn't? "No beating, no confession." Chang
> Ch'ien, beat him!
>
> (Chang does so.)
>
> Wang: I can't stand such torture! I'll make [a] false con-
> fession! Yes sir, I did kill Mr. Liu. . . .
>
> (YCH, pp. 671-72)

It is as simple as that. Only a few moments later, in the prison cell,
Wang is again summoned to the clerk and harassed as before:

> Clerk Chao: Now, where are the two pieces of loot--
> the silk kerchief with sesame print and the ring of
> alloyed silver?
>
> Wang: Brother, I was forced to make a false confession.
> I really don't have them.
>
> Clerk Chao: "No flogging, no confession." Jailor, beat
> him!
>
> (Jailor beats Wang.)
>
> Wang: I can't stand the beating--I'll confess! Yes, yes,
> yes! I put them under the slate by the well in the
> vegetable garden of Liu the Cripple's outside of Hsiao-
> lin township.
>
> (YCH, p. 672)

There is no denying that the two torture scenes have been given short
shrift: it looks as though the playwright knew he had reached a point
where convention was called for and hurriedly disposed of it. In both
instances, the reader simply has to take Wang's word for it (that he
cannot stand the beating) and consider that sufficient explanation for his

fabrication of his own guilt. But then, the same problem may not have confronted the Yüan audience. In a performance, the beatings would take on a much more realistic dimension than suggested by the simple stage direction--"Jailor beats Wang." This observation is substantiated by the comic farmer's firsthand report just a little later in the play: "And, good heavens! [the jailor] kept beating Wang until Wang was soaked with blood through and through. . . ." (YCH, p. 673).

Occasionally, the extortion of a confession is dealt with at greater length, so that one witnesses the victim's emotional or psychological changes. This is the case with Hai-t'ang in Circle:

Hai-t'ang: I have nothing to do with the poisoning of my lord.

Clerk: The obstinacy of a hardened miscreant: "No flogging, no confession." Attendants, drag her down and give her a sound beating!

(The attendants do so.)

Mrs. Ma: Good work! Good work! It would make no difference to me if she should die of a beating.

Clerk: She is feigning death. Lift her up again!

(The attendants do so.)

Hai-t'ang (coming to): Ai-yo! Heaven!

(sings)　　　後庭花 Hou-t'ing hua

The swishing rod falls
Scorching on my back.
My senses are all confused, as though I had collapsed;
My wits forsaking me, slowly.
And they are pulling my hair, so mercilessly.

Servants: Tsk! Confess quick: it's better than going through all this!

Hai-t'ang [goes on singing]:

Shouting and yelling pierces my ears.
Such a wicked clerk--can he ever be forgiven?
Such heartless servants--their brutality and violence shows through.

Clerk: Speak, who's your paramour?

Prefect Su: Since she won't say, let me volunteer for the job!

Hai-t'ang [goes on to sing]:

Forced by the court, I have to
Name a lover and account for his whereabouts.

雙雁兒 <u>Shuang yen-erh</u>

I have been close to the Gates of Ghosts
Two or three times now.
You: how much did you gain by taking bribes?
I: smeared with pus and blood, I swear revenge!
The rich have an easy time always
While the poor can scarce get by at all.

Clerk: Beat her some more!

Hai-t'ang: I was gently reared in a good family: how
can I stand such beatings? I have no other choice
than [to] make [a] false confession. Yes, your
honor, I poisoned by lord, robbed [Mrs. Ma] of
her child, and usurped the family properties. Oh
heaven! What injustice!

(<u>YCH</u>, pp. 1119-20)

With its many details, the scene is apparently far more "realistic"
than those quoted from <u>Kerchief</u>. Hai-t'ang's own description of her
suffering explains eloquently and persuasively why her outlook changes
from optimism (after all, <u>she</u> elected the settlement in court) to utter
desperation, in which hope is given up. There is greater psychological
truth in Hai-t'ang's compliance than in Wang Hsiao-erh's, who is only
given a one-liner, as it were, in comparable scenes.

Yet we must not forget that Hai-t'ang's is <u>the</u> leading role throughout the play. At her disposal are not merely spoken lines of prose but
elevated arias--a privilege not enjoyed by the likes of Wang Hsiao-erh,
who in <u>his</u> play is but a minor character. (More on this distinction when
we take up the leading role later.) Besides--and this is more important--
if Wang's confession and Hai-t'ang's are different in style, they are
nevertheless of the same order. Both Wang and Hai-t'ang, like their
counterparts in the other five plays, are stock characters acting out
their accepted role in conventional situations. Their role in this case
is that of a victim doubly injured: by the lawless crook on one hand
and by the unscrupulous law-enforcer on the other. The fact that a
victim like Wang Hsiao-erh looks unconvincing to the sophisticated
reader of today would not have bothered the Yüan dramatist at all. One
of the wonders that stage convention is capable of working is the willing
suspension of disbelief on the part of the audience. The playwright
obviously knew how to manipulate this suspension with <u>his</u> audience, and
<u>his</u> audience, not later readers, was all the playwright was concerned
about.

The judge

The other prominent figure, a familiar face, in every courtroom play is of course the judge. The word "judge," as used throughout this paper, applies not only to the chief official of a local yamen--a magistrate or a prefect--who is supposed to discharge both executive and judicial duties, but also refers to his subordinate, the clerk, who serves in so many kung-an plays as the de facto justice. In the judgment reversal group, there are necessarily two types of judges: first comes the venal, to be followed by the honest. As has been noted earlier, it is the inevitable hard lot of the victim in these plays to suffer, in addition to being framed and bullied by the villain, further tortures and indignities at the hands of the unconscionable judge to whom he has, ironically, appealed for justice. The tables are turned when the upright judge arrives to set everything straight.

The portrait of the first set of judges is characterized by two features: venality and incompetence. As with the other characters, these qualities are brought forth in explicit terms. A convenient vehicle for such purposes is again the entrance verse, usually doggerel, recited by the judge himself. In Doll, for instance, the prefect appears on stage with these lines:

> When I'm the judge I hear each plea
> With fine impartiality.
> I take my gold with an open mind
> From defense and plaintiff equally.
> The senior judge would (if he knew)
> Flog me till the cocks all crew.
>
> (YCH, p. 1375)[8]

Coming on stage shortly afterwards is the prefect's clerk, who, as if to demonstrate his compatibility with his boss, has his piece of verse:

> The judge is clean as water,
> His clerk, white as flour;
> When the two are mixed together,
> You're in for a muddled picture.
>
> (YCH, pp. 1375-76)

Almost to a word, these same stanzas are to be heard from the law enforcers in Rescue (YCH, p. 767) and Child (YCH, p. 568). They also surface in the other plays couched in slightly different phrases.[9] The example from Circle should suffice to illustrate the point (it is Prefect "Soft" Su speaking):

> Although a judge, of law
> I'm plainly ignorant;
> But he who offers me silver
> Shall be acquitted innocent.

(YCH, p. 1116)

Their words speak of incompetence and their actions prove it. In Doll and Injustice, the prefect/judge falls on his knees when the clerk gives the order (to the plaintiff) to kneel; and to his attendants who are dumbfounded by such impropriety he explains, "How little you know! Whoever comes to court and makes complaint is my daily bread for which I have great respect" (YCH, pp. 1375, 1507)! Quite as often, the titular head of the yamen, because of his oafishness, displays "great respect" for his underlings. As a matter of fact, except in Injustice and Hairpins, most chief officials of the local government profess their inability to handle the lawsuit and have to delegate judicial responsibility to their subordinates. The example from Child may be an extreme one but serves well to illustrate the abjectness of the blockheaded official. There the magistrate, having heard the plaintiff, decides: "It's a case of homicide--how in the world am I to solve it?" Ergo, he summons his clerk.

Chang Ch'ien: The clerk is here, your honor.

Magistrate: Would he please come in?

Chang Ch'ien: This way, please.

Clerk (greeting the magistrate): What is your pleasure, your honor?

Magistrate (greeting the clerk on his knees): Dear clerk, I wouldn't have troubled you if I didn't need your help. Someone's come with a murder case and I can't solve it; so I called you to judge for me.

Clerk: Get up, please. It would be disgraceful if this should be seen by other people. . . .

(YCH, p. 568)

The less-than-dignified official is often caught in other unseemly postures as well. The prefect in <u>Kerchief</u>, while holding a court session, goes out of his way to thank his clerk for the wine feast that "caused [his] stomach to ache the whole night through." The boss's deportment on stage at this point must have been most unbecoming, for his clerk has to admonish him thus, "Sit down, my lord!--The riffraff are watching!" (<u>YCH</u>, p. 671) Similarly, the prefect in <u>Circle</u> is remonstrated by his attendants when, mistaking her social status, he becomes indecorously courteous to the plaintiff (<u>YCH</u>, pp. 1116-17). Yet by far the most irreverent version of the convention to mock and humiliate the chief official is found in the first trial scene of <u>Rescue</u>. The magistrate there, on his mission to encourage agriculture, finds himself confronted with a murder case filed by an elderly woman. The following episode is what in part ensues:

Magistrate: What is your complaint?

Woman: A murder case it is.

Magistrate: Brother clerk, let's go home! She is filing
a case of murder: don't you get me into it!

Clerk: Never mind, your honor. I know how to handle
it.

Magistrate: Whatever you say. Chang Ch'ien, take my
horse. . . .

(All people concerned are brought in.)

Magistrate: Brother clerk, don't tell me you didn't just
let a fart!

Clerk: No, it's not me!

Magistrate: I'll smell and decide <u>that</u> for myself! . . .
So, indeed it wasn't you!--Oh, it's the smell of the
corpse over there in the woods. Brother clerk,
you go ahead and interrogate. I'll keep quiet now.

(<u>YCH</u>, p. 764)

The ludicrous picture of the magistrate stooping down to make his judicial "decision" is not what one would expect of a judge, but it is everything the convention (and a lusty audience) could ask for. On one hand, the cowardice (among other things) of the fainthearted official is the direct opposite of the insolence of the bumptious, boldfaced villain; on the other, his nonchalant and apathetic air contrasts with the agonies suffered by the victim.

But the obtuse official cannot go far, even in his wrong doing, without the able assistance of his emboldened underling. Indeed, behind almost every contemptible, scatterbrained magistrate is most assuredly an equally contemptible but shrewder clerk. Greater familiarity with legal niceties makes the clerk much more efficient than his boss. In the final analysis, however, the two share equally a love of money, disregard for law, and unconcern for human life--to name but a few sterling qualities. For the archetype let us turn to Clerk Sung in Child, who has taken charge of a murder case at the request of his boss.

> Clerk Sung: Hey, you--which one of you is the plaintiff?
>
> Li Te-yi: Me, sir, the Second of the Li's.
>
> Clerk Sung (taking a close look [at him]): Well, this fellow-- haven't I seen him before? Oh yes, oh yes. The other day, while patrolling, I stopped by his door and asked for a seat, but he refused to oblige me. My boy, now you've made your way to this yamen of mine! Chang Ch'ien, lift him over here!
>
> Chang Ch'ien: Yes, sir.
>
> (Li Te-yi mimes handing over silver and sticking out three fingers.)
>
> Clerk Sung (looking carefully): What's wrong with those other two fingers of yours--rotted? Now you cut that out and deliver all [the money] this evening.
>
> Now you, which one is the plaintiff and which one the defendant? You there: where do you come from? What is your name? What is your complaint? Give me the truthful account! If what you say is reasonable, I'll let you off; if not, I'll give you a sound beating!
>
> Li Te-yi: Have pity, sir. This is my sister-in-law, who has a secret paramour. And this old one knows about it all. The woman caused my brother to die of anger and she also murdered my nephew. Good clerk, be my advocate!
>
> Clerk Sung: So it's a murder case. It seems to me the woman is a bad one. Chang Ch'ien, bring the woman forth!

Woman! How did you drive your husband to apoplexy and murder your own child? Tell me the truth.

A-Ch'en: I didn't kill my husband, nor did I murder my own child.

Clerk Sung: "No flogging, no confession." Chang Ch'ien, give her a good beating!

Chang Ch'ien: Confess! (He beats her.)

Clerk Sung: Take the woman to one side. Bring that old fellow forward.

Chang Ch'ien: Yes sir.

Clerk Sung: Old fellow, it seems "the stealing of cold and delivering of warmth"* has been your business, old scoundrel! Chang Ch'ien, give him a sound beating.

Chang Ch'ien (as he beats him): Confess quick! . . .

(YCH, pp. 568-69)

Sure enough, by the end of the act A-Ch'en has confessed to both charges. In the able hands of the no-nonsense clerk, the case has drawn to a swift and, as far as the clerk and his boss are concerned, successful close. It is on the timely arrival of the good honest judge that the victim has now to pin her hopes.

One expects the second set of judges to be of a different stripe completely. (After all, are they not the ones to right the wrongs and overturn the scandalous verdict reached earlier by their corrupt and incompetent colleagues?) The expectation is met, but only in part. The distinction between judges of the first trial and those of the second actually centers around such issues as integrity and attitude. Whereas the former are venal, grasping, and frivolous, the latter are characterized by uncompromised austerity and dead seriousness. These traits, too, are quickly made apparent from the judges' entrance verses. In Hairpins, for instance, Judge Chang recites on his second appearance:

Read The Odes to know the nation well

---

* The context suggests that the phrase t'ou-han sung-nuan 偷寒送暖 describes the activities of a secret go-between or a pimp.

And study the I Ching to learn of Heaven's will.
My brush exhorts the loyal and filial,
My sword is ready to behead the illegal.

(WP, p. 192)

The moral sense and the concern for justice are even more explicit in
Wang Hsiao-jan's verse in Rescue:

By imperial laws
The corrupt official loses his head;
A clean, fairminded one
Brings peace to the public instead.
When injustice plagues
The populace,
The sword of power, the golden badge
Must be lifted from disgrace.

(YCH, p. 771)

In the last piece the picture of sternness is further enhanced by the in-
vocation of the sword of authority and the golden badge, both of which
are imperial symbols of supreme judicial power enabling their bearer
"to execute first and memorialize afterwards." In all but two (Child
and Hairpins) of the judgment reversal plays, these emblems are mentioned.

The most unequivocal statement on the integrity and seriousness
of the second judge is found in a speech (in Circle) by Pao Cheng, the
most austere (except when he appears in Selling Relief Grains in Ch'en-
chou [Ch'en-chou t'iao-mi 陳州糶米 , YCH #3], where he is appealingly
human) of all judges in Yüan courtroom dramas; the following translation
is George A. Hayden's:[10]

(in verse)

Years ago I received my emperor's commission.
My hands grasp the golden badge and the sword of
authority.
Everyone speaks of the Southern Court and its Hall
of Retribution;
No need have we for the Eastern Mountain and its
Tower of Purgatory.

[in prose]

My surname is Pao, my given name Cheng, and
my courtesy name Hsi-wen. I come from Lao-erh
Hamlet, Ssu-wang Village, Chin-tou-chün, Lu-chou.

I am honest, capable, pure, and upright, staunch
and firm in my integrity. I am eager in service to my
country and scornful of devotion to money. I associate
only with loyal and filial men and have nothing to do
with slanderers and flatterers.

Thanks be to his Majesty for his favor and mercy
in granting me the positions of Academician-in-waiting
of the Lung-t'u Pavilion and Scholar of the T'ien-chang
Pavilion. I now have the post of prefect of the Southern
Court in K'ai-feng-fu.

By imperial gift I hold the sword of authority and
the golden badge, with which to investigate corrupt
officials and dishonest clerks and to undo the grievances
and right the wrongs of the common people. I have
permission to execute first and report afterward.

The rich and powerful families therefore have
only to hear my name and they fold their hands. The
cruel and wicked see my shadow and there is none
whose heart does not turn cold.

Outside my boundary sign I have tied ropes into a
stockade; by my barrier wall I have marked the ground
for a jail.* "Officials [be]** orderly and dignified,"
the emperor's calligraphy is carved on the admonition
stone. The attendants are stern, and beneath the court
steps are written the two words "Voices low." In the
shade of the green locust trees are arranged twenty-

---

* The virtue of the Ancient Sage Kings was said to be so great that they
had only to draw a circle on the ground around a malefactor and it made
an inescapable jail.--Perng.

** Hayden has "Officials are . . . " but I think the injunctive mood
approximates the original closer, the phrase kuan-liao cheng-su 官僚
整肅 being the emperor's admonition.

four magpie-tail long cangues; before the Hall of
Benevolent Rule are laid several hundred wolf-tooth
large staves.

(in verse)

Throughout the day no dust reaches the Yellow Hall;
Only the locusts' shade encroaches on the paths.
Who among outsiders dares make a clamor?
When passing by, even the crows do not caw. . . .

(YCH, pp. 1124-25)

Nevertheless, while the review judge's austerity and seriousness
of purpose can be established in this way, his intelligence or capacity
to solve the case remains for him a real test in which, indeed, he seldom receives high marks. The truth of the matter is that most of the
judges of the second trial are nearly as incompetent as their corrupt
counterparts: both rely heavily on intuition, and all routinely resort
to torture. Above (pp. 102-3) we witnessed Clerk Sung, a most insensate justice, working hard on his case. The following episode is taken
from the same play (Child), but this time it is the famous Judge Pao
reviewing the identical case in the second trial.

Judge Pao: You there, say your complaint.

Li Te-yi: My brother is Li Te-jen; I am Li Te-yi. My
sister-in-law has a lover. She caused my brother to
die of anger and she also murdered my nephew. Be
my advocate, your honor!

Judge Pao: Which one is Li A-Ch'en?

Li A-Ch'en: That's me.

Judge Pao: You, Li A-Ch'en, answer my questions:

(sings)   慶東原 Ch'ing tung-yuan

Whose idea was it to compete for the family inheritance?

Li A-Ch'en: It's my brother-in-law's.

Judge Pao: Did you hear that, Li Te-yi?

(sings)

Who caused your husband to die of anger?

Li A-Ch'en: It's my brother-in-law again.

Judge Pao: Did you hear that, Li Te-yi?

(sings)

So it was the intemperance of this fellow
That drove his own brother to apoplexy!

Li Te-yi: Your honor, I had nothing to do with it! It's all
my sister-in-law here. She could not get along with
any of her relatives; she caused my brother to die of
anger; she strangled my nephew--she did them all!

Judge Pao: (sings)

Did you say, she was ill-disposed toward all her
relatives?

Li Te-yi: If you don't believe me, sir, you may ask the
neighbors.

Judge Pao: (sings)

Silence! Is there need, indeed, to ask the neighbors?

(says) Li Te-yi, if you don't confess,

(sings)

I'll give you a beating so harsh that you may die of
it! . . .

(YCH, p. 572)

Beyond a doubt Judge Pao espouses the same judicial philosophy as
Clerk Sung's; neither manifests any qualms about making use of torture
to get at the truth as each conceives it. The only distinction lies in the
following: instinctively, Judge Pao and many other judges of the review
trial take sides with the victim--almost at their first glimpse of the latter. On the other hand, Clerk Sung and his colleagues in the first trial,
spurred by mercenary interest (implicit or explicit),[11] lose no time in
joining hands with the knave. This distinction is a significant one. By
contrast, the image of the honest judge as insightful or compassionate
is considerably enhanced.

Intuition and the resort to physical torture aid the good judge--
but only to a certain point. The sly villain and the wicked official prove
a lot tougher to deal with than the simple, artless victim. As a result,
tricks and supernatural interventions are de rigueur in the review trial.
In Child, for instance, Judge Pao is finally able to bring justice to the

case, thanks to the ghost of Shen-nu-erh, who appears in court to become his own advocate. The same thing happens in Injustice: at the request of her father (who, though endowed with the conventional sword of authority and golden badge, remains an ineffectual justice), Tou Ngo descends in spirit form to defend her good name against Donkey Chang and succeeds in pinning down the true culprit. The deus ex machina type of dénouement is found in two other plays--Hairpins and Rescue. In the former, the timely arrival of the innkeeper who has on his own initiative captured the true murderer, straightens things out for the two baffled judges. In Rescue, the supposedly deceased wife of Yang Hsing-tsu returns home safe and sound in the nick of time to rescue her brother-in-law from the gallows as well as from shame. Kerchief and Doll are the only two plays where the conduct of the review trial is delegated to a clever and honest clerk. In each he displays great intelligence and ingenuity in discovering the truth; each, nevertheless, after the truth is known, needs to rely on a trick to conclude the case formally. The single exception in this regard is Circle, where Judge Pao's success must be attributed not to any trick or supernatural intervention, but to his discernment.[12]

A dénouement of this kind cannot enhance the image or characterization of the honest judge involved; if anything, it reflects badly on his ability to discern the truth. It carries the serious implication that as far as competence or mental acuteness goes, the judge of the review trial is not much superior to the judge of the mistrial; indeed, one is just as fallible as the other. This, coupled with the fact that both rely heavily and indiscriminately on physical torture to extort confession, tends to equate the two sets of judges. The fallibility of the good judge, as George A. Hayden points out, may serve two purposes: to take the audience by surprise and to keep his characterization within mortal bounds.[13] Both are dramaturgical concerns. The tricks and supernatural elements that abound in the second trial, furthermore, were certainly used to secure immediate theatrical effects.

The above synthesis seems to suggest a current of the comic running beneath the Yüan dramatist's manipulation of stock characters: however serious and gruesome the business at hand, the villain, the victim, and the judge never fail to bring with them moments of relief, laughter, and buffoonery. This comic quality is achieved in large measure by means of bold exaggeration and caricature so often found in their characterization. Exaggeration and caricature, again, are products of the theatrical urge; subtlety appears to have been deliberately shunned in favor of the more immediate success in the playhouse. This preference may seem to indicate the presence of an unsophisticated audience, but that is really beside the point. Furthermore, it is a relative thing--certainly the musical sophistication of the Yüan tsa-chü audience was impressive; we are simply unable to measure it because of all the arts music perishes most easily.

The Case of the Leading Role

Our observation of the conventions involved in the maneuvering of the major stock characters may give the impression that dramatis personae in Yüan tsa-chü are static and flat and do not develop. Though this is true in most cases (especially when those in question play supporting roles), exceptions must be made for the leading character, who is, after all, quite a different species from his colleagues. In tsa-chü, prose and verse are shared in common by all the players, but in any given act the leading role alone sings the arias. And the aria is an effective means to bring out the inner, subtler feelings or emotions of the singer (see p. 21ff.). We have seen that the portrait of Hai-t'ang (Circle) as a victimized character is at once more valid and more convincing than that of Wang Hsiao-erh (Kerchief), who is also a victim. Playing the lead, Hai-t'ang has at her command an eloquent and forceful tool of expression, the aria; in addition to the general traits shared by all victims, an individual, more human, side is strikingly presented in lyrics to the accompaniment of music. The study of conventions would not be complete without reference to the custom of a single singing role and how it affects characterization.

To illustrate, let us take Tou Ngo in Injustice. A critic has recently observed, quite correctly, that Tou Ngo is the very incarnation of the traditional Chinese notion of ethics or morality.[14] What he has failed to recognize is that Tou Ngo is also something else: she is a human being, made of flesh and blood, goaded as well by passion and mortal urges.[15] In the following discussion I have no wish to treat Tou Ngo as a tragic heroine in the Western sense of the term.[16] She is not-- as indeed none in Yüan tsa-chü ever is. Yet, while she may not in every way meet the requirements of a "round" character, Tou Ngo in Injustice is far from being a "flat" personality--thanks to her leading role. Except in the capsule "Prologue," where her father has one very short aria, Tou Ngo sings the lead throughout the play and is given numerous touching lyrics, particularly in the first three acts. It is in these lyrics that a complex and very human Tou Ngo should be discovered.

Since the cosmic images in the arias of Act III and the way they bear on Tou Ngo's stature as victim have been dealt with in the previous chapter (p. 42ff.), the present discussion will focus on the lyrics of Acts I and II.

The misfortune of Tou Ngo, a victim of blind fate, forms the heart of the matter in the "Prologue." We see the half-orphaned child, at seven, virtually sold by her own father to Granny Ts'ai, his creditor, in return for fifty taels of silver. What transpired during the next thirteen long years is related by Granny Ts'ai, now Tou Ngo's mother-in-law, when Act I has barely begun:[17]

> Since that time thirteen years ago when Scholar Tou T'ien-chang left his daughter Tuan-yün behind to be my daughter-in-law, I have changed her name to Tou Ngo. Not quite two years after the marriage, my son died suddenly of consumption. My daughter-in-law has already been a widow for three years, and will soon be out of mourning. . . .
>
> (YCH, p. 1500)[18]

The same message is repeated in the next scene--with a small but noticeable distinction. This time it is Tou Ngo herself speaking, and we find the complete detachment in Granny Ts'ai's narration replaced by bitterness, although muffled and restrained at first:

> My family name is Tou; my humble name is Tuan-yün. My ancestor came from Ch'u-chou. When I was three, I lost my mother; at seven I was separated from my father. He gave me away to Mistress Ts'ai to be her daughter-in-law, and she changed my name to Tou Ngo. When I reached the age of seventeen, I was married. Unfortunately my husband died, and it has already been three years. Now I am twenty years old. . . . Ah, Tou Ngo, this life of yours, how miserable! . . .
>
> (YCH, p. 1501)[19]

The grumbling comes from one who has every reason to be disenchanted with life. The voice is low yet clear.

Although bitterness is apparent in her recounting of the past, the main thrust of Tou Ngo's complaint is about the present. The depressing widowhood that she has to endure constitutes the single most unbearable fact in life, as the following lyrics suggest:

點絳唇 Tien chiang-ch'un

Of my heart full of sorrow,
Of my years of suffering,
Is Heaven aware?
If Heaven only knew my situation,
Would it not also grow thin?

混江龍 Hun-chiang lung

I just want to ask:
To go without eating or sleep both day and night--
When is this to end?
What appears in last night's dream often lingers in
    the mind today.
Embroidered flowers lying across the door call forth
    tears;
The full moon hanging above the lady's chamber breaks
    one's heart.
I have long been anxious and unable to suppress my
    yearning;
Deeply depressed, I cannot relax my knitted brows.
More and more my heart grows heavy,
And my thoughts wander about and become long.

(YCH, p. 1501)[20]

Here is a youthful widow protesting a loneliness that is suffocating and
destructive.[21] The irrepressible yearning for love haunts her day and
night, costing her peace of mind. Even the sights of "embroidered
flowers lying across the door" (in all probability this refers to the door
hanging. Cf. Shih (I), p. 77, note on the character t'a 闥 : "door of an
inner room"; "a hanging above a door") and "the full moon hanging
above the lady's chamber" prove too much for her to bear--undoubtedly
because they quickly and unavoidably evoke associations of a happy,
romantic nuptial life. The "injustice" suffered by Tou Ngo dates back
to her early childhood, but it is now, as a vaguely awakened young
widow, that she finds it most unbearable.

An appreciation of the widow's longing for the impossible--a fulfilled marital life--is crucial to the understanding of Tou Ngo's idiosyncracy and behavior. Indeed, her preoccupation with conjugal love takes
on the precarious proportion of a fixed idea; her language abounds in
images denoting or connoting various aspects of marriage. This is
especially pronounced in the first two acts. Take, for instance, her

reactions to the marriage proposals of the Changs. When Granny Ts'ai professes that she is being bothered by Old Chang who desires her hand in marriage (in return for saving her life), Tou Ngo's advice as a daughter is dutiful and decorously sensible. "Mother-in-law," she begins by saying, "this, I fear, won't do. You should reconsider: we are not starving, nor lacking in clothes, nor in debt and hard-pressed by creditors. Besides, you're advanced in age: you're over sixty now. How could you take another husband?" (YCH, p. 1502) But, when Granny Ts'ai appears perfectly willing to go along with the bullies' demand and, more importantly, when she reveals further that she has also pledged Tou Ngo to Donkey Chang, the tone of the daughter-in-law is immediately changed. In the ensuing arias she reprimands Granny Ts'ai first with common sense:

後庭花 Hou-t'ing hua

To avoid evil spirits, one must select auspicious days;
For a wedding ceremony, one must offer incense-
    burning.
Now your knot of hair is as white as snow,
How can you wear the colorful silk veil?
No wonder people say,
You cannot keep a grown girl at home.
Now you are about sixty years of age,
Isn't it said that "when middle age arrives, all is
    over"?
With one stroke, you mark off the memories of former
    love;
Now you and this man act like newlyweds.
To no purpose you make people split their mouths
    with laughter.

She then torments her with memories of the past and reminds her of her moral obligations:

青哥兒 Ch'ing-ko-erh

Though indeed you had him, had him save you,
You are no longer young like a bamboo shoot, like
    a bamboo shoot;
How can you paint your eyebrows fine to make another
    match?
Your husband left you his property;
He made plans for you;
He bought fertile land to provide food for morning and
    evening

And clothing for summer and winter,
Fully expecting his widowed wife and orphaned son
To remain free and independent till old age.
Oh, father-in-law, you labored in vain!

She also taunts her with sarcasm:

寄生草 Chi-sheng ts'ao

You say that he is excited and happy.
I, however, am worried for your sake.
I worry that you, in waning spirit, cannot swallow
  the nuptial wine;
I worry that you, with failing vision, cannot tie the
  love-knot of congenial hearts;
I worry that you, sleepy and feeling dim, cannot rest
  secure under the flower-quilt.
You want to be led by songs and music to the wedding
  hall;
I would say this match will certainly lag behind others.

(YCH, pp. 1502-3)[22]

The theme these arias harp on is the same that has Tou Ngo's
mind possessed: marriage. This preoccupation is understandable, for
traditionally the lives of unmarried women and particularly of widows
were miserable--as the present situation of Granny Ts'ai and Tou Ngo
demonstrates. More importantly, marriage is the proper theme for
the occasion: Granny Ts'ai has just brought up the prospect of marrying
themselves to the Changs. Nevertheless, the ready and orderly fashion
in which Tou Ngo delivers her train of thoughts seems to confirm our
previous impression and points to her preoccupation. The content of her
lecture is all that may be expected from a woman of her status and mentality: folk sayings, conventional notions, and trite expressions. Significantly, Tou Ngo's general remarks on marriage narrow down in
focus in the last aria. The nuptial wine, the love-knot of congenial
hearts, and the flower-quilt are images suggestive of marital consum-
mation--the warmth of bed denied to Tou Ngo as a widow.

The discourse on the matrimonial relationship is resumed in
Act II with historical allusions aplenty. By this time the Changs have
already moved into the Ts'ai abode and, perturbed by such an arrangement, Tou Ngo reflects to herself in a miniature monologue:

Mother-in-law, we widows should be discreet in all things.
How can we keep Donkey Chang and his father, who are not

114

relatives or members of our family, here in the house with
us? Won't that make people talk? Mother-in-law, do not
promise them your hand secretly and involve me also in
impropriety. I can't help thinking how hard it is to keep
watch over a woman's heart. . . .

Along the same line she goes on contemplating the fickleness of women
as well as their love of carnal pleasure--even outside of wedlock:

一枝花 Yi-chih hua

She wants to rest behind love-bird curtains all her
    life,
Unwilling to sleep in an empty chamber for half a
    night.
First she was Mr. Chang's spouse, now she is
    Mr. Li's wife.
There are some women, who, following each other's
    fashion,
Speak not of household matters, but pick up all idle
    gossip.
They talk ambiguously of catching-phoenix adventures,
And display knowledge of trapping-dragon tricks.

梁州第七 Liang-chou ti-ch'i

"This one is like Lady Chao, who worked in a tavern;[1]
"This, like Meng Kuang, who raised her tray as high
    as her eyebrows."[2]
Behind these words they cleverly hide their true selves.
Their words do not reveal; their deeds give them away.
Old love is easily forgotten, in favor of new.
The earth on the grave-mound is still moist, and
New clothes are already hanging on the rack.

---

[1] Lady Chao (Wen-chün) was wife to Ssu-ma Hsiang-ju (179-117 B.C.).
"When they were poor, they kept a small tavern in Ch'eng-tu, where
she served as a barmaid"--Shih (I), p. 137.

[2] "Meng was the wife of Liang Hung of the Later Han. She showed her
respect and love [for her husband] by bringing in the dinner tray as
high as her eyebrows . . ." (Ibid.).

Where could one find a woman who would weep down the
  Great Wall at her husband's funeral?[3]
Where could one find a washing maid willing to plunge
  into the high water?[4]
Where could one find a wife turned into stone while
  waiting for her husband's return?[5]
It's a pity, nay, a shame, that women are no longer
  virtuous
But wanton and lacking in purpose!
The exemplars are not observed;
"Human nature is hard to change"--oh, how true![6]

(YCH, p. 1505)[23]

---

[3] ". . . Meng Chiang-nü, whose husband . . . died while a conscript
laborer working on the Great Wall . . . went to seek her husband
and wept so bitterly at the foot of the wall that part of it crumbled
and exposed her husband's body" (Ibid., p. 139).

[4] "During the Spring and Autumn period, the minister Wu Tzu-hsü
fled from the state of Ch'u to Wu. A woman washing by the river
took pity on the refugee and fed him. . . . [Later] she drowned herself in the river to assure him that no word of his escape could come
from her. Another reason for her drowning was that although she
helped the refugee out of compassion, she nevertheless failed in
chastity in dealing with a man who was a stranger . . ." (Ibid.).

[5] "This refers to a legend that a faithful wife, during her husband's
absence from home, climbed a hill every day to watch for his return, until finally she was transformed into a large stone . . ."
(Ibid.).

[6] The last two lines in Shih's version read, "Fortunately, there were
faithful women of old;/Thus say not that human nature is hard to
change." She adds, in a note, "Here it means: 'Do not say that
women are born to be fickle, because many women in the old days
were chaste and faithful'"--Shih (I), p. 139. Her interpretation
(particularly of the last line), however, seems inconsistent with--
or at least does damage to--the pervading sense of moral indignation
and outrage that has been gradually generated up to this point.

By invoking the illustrious women of the past, the passage is crammed with didactic implications; it sounds more like Morality itself preaching uxorial virtues than an obedient daughter pleading her case. On the other hand, the two arias may be a just reflection of Tou Ngo's state of mind. In the first, Yi-chih hua, she talks boldly and freely about "sleeping behind love-bird curtains" and "empty chamber" at night. There is even mention of the possibilities of extramarital adventures ("catching phoenixes and trapping dragons").[24] In the second lyric, Liang-chou ti-ch'i, she enumerates those renowned wives whose spiritual bonds with their husbands were indivisible. Together, the two arias stress the two essential aspects of married life: physical love and spiritual love. They are consistent with the characterization of a lovelorn widow who aspires to both but can attain neither.

This leads us to the appraisal of Tou Ngo's submission to the pressure of Judge T'ao in the first trial. There Donkey Chang, cleverly imputing the murder of his father to Tou Ngo, insinuates that "this woman, though young, is extremely hardened and stubborn, unafraid of beatings." The timely suggestion prompts the complacent judge to take note of the fact that "people are mean worms: if you don't beat them, they will never confess." He immediately orders a harsh flogging ("Attendants, select a heavy stick and beat her!"), during which the court attendants three times have to sprinkle water on Tou Ngo to revive her (YCH, pp. 1507-8). Thus, like the other victimized characters, Tou Ngo suffers unspeakable agonies in court. Unlike them, however, she remains firm and does not yield under physical torture. She protests the injustice and inhumanity:

罵玉郎 Ma Yü-lang

This heartless stick is more than I can endure.
Oh mother, this indeed is your own doing;
Who else can be blamed?

. . . .

感皇恩 Kan huang-en

Ah! Who is shouting so fiercely?
I cannot help being frightened out of my wits.
No sooner does the noise stop and I begin to revive,
Than once again I faint.
A thousand beatings and ten thousand punishments;
For each blow that falls--one streak of blood, one
    layer of skin!

採茶歌 Ts'ai-ch'a ko

They beat me till pieces of my flesh fly off,
And I am dripping with blood.
Who can know the bitterness in my heart?
. . . .
Oh Heaven, why don't the sun's rays
　　Ever reach underneath an overturned tub?

(YCH, p. 1508)[25]

And still she does not give in. To the impatient judge's menacing question, "Are you confessing or not?" Tou Ngo replies simply: "Indeed I did not poison him" (YCH, p. 1508).

With Tou Ngo, the convention of the change of heart is brought about through a different route. Unable to bend the frail woman's will, the persistent judge decides to try his luck on Granny Ts'ai for a change. "Since you are not the one," he reasons, "beat that old hag!" Upon hearing this, Tou Ngo instantly changes her position:

Stop, stop, stop! Don't touch my mother-in-law! Rather,
let me confess: I did poison my [step-] father-in-law. . . .

(YCH, p. 1508)

After so much ado, her surrender at this point seems abrupt and puzzling. Up to this moment she has courageously--and quite effectively--frustrated the unscrupulous official's brutal strategy. Why should she yield now? The handy explanation that Tou Ngo herself advances in the next aria (黃鐘尾 Huang-chung wei) is:

Oh mother, if I don't die,
How can you be saved?

(YCH, p. 1508)

This rationale is consistent with her report, later, to the review justice who happens to be her long-absent father: "Yet when the prefect saw that your child would not comply, he turned to my mother-in-law and was going to torture her. I was afraid that she, an aged woman, could not stand the torture; I had no other alternative than to confess to the false charge" (YCH, p. 1514). What Tou Ngo has done appears to be a simple and noble act of self-sacrifice.

The problem with such a theory is that it is too pat. Filial piety as a virtue occupies an uncontested niche in the Chinese mentality, and what could be more desirable and appropriate, and command more respect, than the fact that a daughter rushes to the rescue of her aging mother-in-law, knowing full well the fatal consequences of such an act? By attributing Tou Ngo's defeat solely to a brand of filial piety that borders on the inhuman, we reduce a complex human personality to a single, simple idea. Having seen the young widow struggle with comprehensible desires, one is left with the question: was her choice of death nothing but a response to filial piety? Does it not relate, in some way, to her miserable fate? In other words, how reliable is Tou Ngo's professed motivation to sacrifice herself for her mother-in-law?

This is not to question Tou Ngo's filial piety, which is convincingly (perhaps overly so) established in the following scene in the third act:

[Tou Ngo is on her way to the execution ground.]

倘秀才 T'ang hsiu-ts'ai

Tou Ngo (sings):

. . . .
Tou Ngo would like to have a word with you, brother.

Executioner: What do you have to say?

Tou Ngo (sings):

If we take the main street, I'll bear you a grudge;
If we take the back alley, I'll die with no regret.
Do not tell me that the back alley is a longer route. . . .

Executioner: Why is that?

Tou Ngo (sings):   叨叨令 Tao-tao ling

. . . .
I fear only that I may be seen by my mother-in-law
    In the main street.

Executioner: You have your own life to worry about now--
    why should you fear being seen?

Tou Ngo (says): If my mother-in-law should see me go in
    cangue and lock to the execution ground and embrace
    the sword,

(sings)

It would just drive her mad!
It would just drive her mad!
Please, brother, do a favor for somone in face
of peril. . . .

(YCH, p. 1509)

Yet Tou Ngo is more than an advocate for filial piety. She is also, as
we have seen, a youthful widow "full of sorrow" and with "years of suffering." The idiosyncracy of her language shows that she is preoccupied
with the emotional as well as spiritual aspect of fulfilled conjugal love,
and the impossibility of attaining it severely damages her morale. Her
rationalization of all this is marked by typical pessimism and submis-
siveness:

油葫蘆 Yu hu-lu

Is it my fate, to be unhappy all my life?
Who but I know such endless grief?
We all know that human feelings, unlike water, cannot
flow endlessly. . . .

天下樂 T'ien-hsia lo

Is it because I burned too little incense in my last
life,
That in this life I have to suffer?
I urge one and all to do good deeds to insure a better
next life.
I will serve my mother-in-law and mourn my husband:
To show I mean what I say.

(YCH, pp. 1501-2)[26]

If there remains for Tou Ngo any hope at all, it lies not in this life but
in the next.

The passage quoted above indicates a tendency in Tou Ngo toward
self-destruction--after all, there is nothing she can possibly lose since
she is doomed to death in any case. It also puts her filial piety in an
entirely different perspective: the cultivation of her own karma is very
much on her mind too. These are incompatible goals, and it may not
be farfetched to suggest that, prior to the first trial, Tou Ngo's behavior reflects a perplexed state of mind in face of such a quandary.

The court decision to torture her mother-in-law suddenly offers her a
way out: by sacrificing herself she can end this life, which she tells us
is meaningless, and help secure for herself a better next life which is
all she can--and does--look forward to. Death for Tou Ngo is a blessing
in thin disguise.

From the foregoing I hope it is clear that, while it does not exactly
"grow" in the play, Tou Ngo's character does display human complexity.
She is not just another conventional victim with merely conventional
attributes. Such complexity is only possible in the leading role, which
equips the actor with the tool of the aria--a potent medium for expressing subtle feelings. The possibilities of the aria role are exploited in
most of the other judgment reversal plays as well: Scholar Chao in
Hairpins, Mrs. Li in Rescue, Hai-t'ang in Circle, and Chang Ting in
both Doll and Kerchief are examples of leading roles whose portraits
are more than superficial. The only exception is Child, where, because
the lead is shared by three characters, none becomes a finished portrait; the really dynamic character in that play is a villainess.

The Major "Minors": Three Examples

The case of Tou Ngo illustrates that, as a rule, the leading role
in tsa-chü is that of a star and its performer has sole access to that
subtler, more elegant, and vastly more powerful dramatic tool, the
aria. The convention often results in the star's being more roundly
delineated than his less glamorous colleagues on stage. (The word
"more" must be underscored because, as has been said before, tsa-chü
characters are conceived of in Theophrastian terms and hence all talk
about their "roundness" can only be relative.) Still, there are in our
group of seven plays several striking instances in which a supporting
role ignites the play or even steals the show. Mrs. Ma in Circle, the
Innkeeper (who does not even have a name) in Hairpins, and Kao Shan
the peddler in Doll are outstandingly successful in this respect. In
these three plays, the dramatists seem able to counterbalance the convention of a single star and by doing so add further dimensions to the
drama.

Mrs. Ma and Female Villainy

Three of the seven judgment reversal plays feature a calculating
female archvillainess, under whose shadow the character of her male

accomplice all but disappears. The epitome of female villainy is undoubtedly Mrs. Ma in Circle, but to put things in proper perspective, a
brief description of the other two villainesses is in order. First, La-
mei in Child. The unrelenting wife of Li Te-yi begins by successfully
sowing seeds of discord between her husband and his elder brother, Te-
jen. After the latter has died of anguish over the clash within the family,
she proceeds to plot against Shen-nu-erh, her nephew and sole heir of
the Li families. The opportunity presents itself when one day her husband brings the child home:

(Enter Li Te-yi, drunk and carrying Child.)

Li Te-yi: Wife, I'm drunk. I've brought Shen-nu-erh with
me. Take good care of him. Buy him some nice fruit
and good cake. Don't let him be frightened. I'll take
a rest. (Li mimes falling asleep.)

La-mei: Husband, you're indeed drunk again, aren't you?
Don't worry; go and sleep. [Aside] Now I won't let
this chance slip: while he is asleep, I'll strangle [the
Child]. I know how to take care of him when he sobers
up. . . .

(La-mei mimes strangling the child to death.)

Li Te-yi (miming waking up): Excellent wine! But drunk
though I was, I still had some wits about me. I remember carrying Shen-nu-erh home. Where is he now?
Wife, where is Shen-nu-erh my child?

La-mei: Shen-nu-erh is sleeping over there, look at him.

Li Te-yi (looking at the child): You heartless woman! You
would leave a child asleep on the cold floor! Now what's
wrong with putting him in bed? Woman, why are you so
inconsiderate? (He rises and looks.) Son, get up and
sleep in the bed. (He takes another look.) Ai-yo! Wife,
you savage woman! Shen-nu-erh was the only scion left
to both families [i.e., his and his brother's]--how could
you bring yourself to strangle him to death? When my
sister-in-law comes to demand Shen-nu-erh, how shall
I answer her? A lawsuit seems unavoidable. Let us go
to court now.

La-mei: P'ei! You brought him home and told me to strangle
him. You're the head of the family: how could I defy
your decision? Let me go to court with you. There, if

you say one word, I'll say two; and if you say two, I'll
say ten--until I succeed in putting the blame on you.
Let us go to the court this moment!

Li Te-yi: [Aside] And she is imputing the blame to me!
[To La-mei] What is to be done now?

La-mei: That's easy. Nobody knew that you had brought
him home, so let's bury the brat in the drain ditch.

Li Te-yi: In the ditch? But would it not show on the surface?

La-mei: Cover it up with a slate and pad that with some
dirt and then tamp it with our feet.--Who in the world
could tell? . . .

Li Te-yi: Wife, you're merciless. But when my sister-
in-law comes--you must face her, alone. . . .

(<u>YCH</u>, p. 563)

Taking advantage of the infirmity of her uxorious husband, La-mei, the
mastermind and executioner of the horrible deed, literally coerces him
into becoming her accomplice. All the while, she keeps a cool head
and is in total command of the situation: a striking contrast to Li Te-yi,
the easily intimidated poltroon.

As ruthless as La-mei but perhaps slyer and more sophisticated
is Mrs. Liu in <u>Kerchief</u>. Early in the play, the reader will remember,
a verbal confrontation develops between the wealthy Mr. Liu and Wang
Hsiao-erh, a pauper, over a broken commode. In the heat of argument,
Wang rashly threatens to kill Mr. Liu should they "meet in the back
alley." Mrs. Liu seizes the opportunity to extract from him a warranty
of life:

Mrs. Liu: Listen to him talk! But what he has said he may
well do. I'll demand from him a warranty of life. [To
Wang] If, within one hundred days, [Mr. Liu] should
suffer from even a headache or slight fever, you shall
be held responsible. Beyond one hundred days, you're
free.

Mr. Liu: What's going on?

Mrs. Liu: Wang Hsiao-erh intends to kill you, so I'm demanding from him a warranty of life.

Mr. Liu: Wife, you know he hasn't the courage. . . .

(YCH, p. 670)

What seems at this point much ado about nothing turns out to be the inception of a well-laid murder plot. In the next scene Mrs. Liu brags about her "unclean business" with a Taoist monk whom she later dispatches to kill her husband. The significance of the "commode commotion" emerges in the episode immediately following the slaughter:

> Neighbors: Mrs. Liu, someone--we don't know who--killed your husband!
>
> (Enter Mrs. Liu.)
>
> Mrs. Liu: Neighbors, who killed my husband?
>
> Neighbors: How should we know?
>
> Mrs. Liu: We have no enemies except Wang Hsiao-erh. We'll go to his home and inquire. Here we are.
>
> (She calls. Enter Wang, who greets her.)
>
> Mrs. Liu: All right! You gave the warranty and in less than ten days you killed my husband! Clearly a matter for Imperial law: I shall go to court with you.
>
> Wang: I didn't even step out of my door--how can you charge me with the murder of your husband? Oh, who will be my advocate? (Exeunt.)

(YCH, p. 671)

The turn of events is ironic when one recalls the preceding interlude-- Wang Hsiao-erh's hollow threat, Mrs. Liu's "wifely discretion," and Mr. Liu's unguarded ignorance. Again it is by way of contrast that the essential qualities of the villainess are brought to the fore. Again, too, it is the villainess who schemes while her male assistant merely takes orders. Like La-mei in Child, Mrs. Liu in Kerchief is the prime mover who steers the course of the drama at will--until, that is, the intervention of the review judge, whose dogged adherence to his unfailing instinct, as we have seen, foils even the most adroitly maneuvered pieces of villainy.

Both La-mei and Mrs. Liu are well-drawn characters, consistent in what they do and lively in what they say. The presentation, nevertheless

leaves something to be desired: their pictures emerge largely from
their own accounts and deeds--perfectly legitimate tools for the dramatist, but offering narrow and limited perspectives. Characters so
delineated contrast with the others on stage and thereby gain significance;
but one can only guess how they are perceived and received by the other
characters. The portrait falls short of roundness essential to complete
persuasiveness. In this regard Mrs. Ma in <u>Circle</u> appears to be a
superior specimen in our gallery of female miscreants: the ingredients
constituting the villainy of all vary only in degree, but information about
Mrs. Ma is conveyed through more channels than one. And each time a
message is delivered by herself (that is, through her own words and/or
deeds), it effectively reinforces or modifies our previous impression.

Mrs. Ma is an earthy, lewd, scheming, and hypocritical figure
throughout the play. Her bawdy language, key to the <u>allégresse</u> that
permeates the otherwise grim drama, has been described in some detail (above, p. 63ff.). In what follows we shall concentrate on the
finesse with which she outmaneuvers those around her--especially Hai-
t'ang, the heroine and courtesan-turned-archrival. Even prior to her
entrance Mrs. Ma's name is alluded to in the "Prologue" when Lord Ma,
intent on taking Hai-t'ang as concubine, is negotiating the terms with
Mrs. Chang, Hai-t'ang's "mother":

> Mrs. Chang: But, sir, you have a wife at home. What if
> my daughter gets bullied after being married to you--
> <u>that</u> would be worse than remaining unmarried. This
> is something I have to clear up with you. . . .

> Lord Ma: You may rest assured, ma'am, not only because
> <u>I</u> am not such an unworthy person but because my wife
> isn't either. When your daughter enters my house-
> hold, she shall be as a sister to my wife. . . .

(<u>YCH</u>, p. 1108)

Lord Ma's characterization of his wife as "not an unworthy person"*
should be noted. A glaring contradiction is found in the next scene
where Mrs. Ma paints herself as quite an unworthy person indeed: without the slightest moral compunction she takes considerable delight in

---

* The Chinese, 不是那等人 <u>pu-shih na-teng-jen</u>, literally means "not
that kind of person"; that is, not the jealous and aggressive kind.

boasting of her affair with Clerk Chao (whose sexual endowments please her extremely--see above, p. 64) and in revealing her dark plot against Lord Ma ("I have made up my mind to poison my husband"). In light of Mrs. Ma's own words, her husband's descriptive remark <u>could</u> be taken as a deliberate misrepresentation of the facts so as to improve his bargaining position. Or it may be construed as a blind appraisal of a doting or inattentive husband. More likely, however, Lord Ma is just another victim of his wife's skillful deception.

In fact, Mrs. Ma lets the audience in on her deceptiveness as she makes her first entrance, at the very beginning of Act I. Here is the doggerel stanza she recites:

> My countenance leaves a lot to be desired
> Although most people praise its color;
> The powder and rouge washed off my face
> Would more than supply a beauty parlor!

> (<u>YCH</u>, p. 1108)

After the recital Mrs. Ma goes on to narrate her extramarital adventure with Clerk Chao and unveil the murder scheme. As is generally the case, the entrance verse says a great deal about the speaker; the light-hearted piece conveys more than just self-mockery. We recognized in the last chapter (p. 63ff.), for instance, the significance of this particular stanza with respect to the theme of reality versus appearance. On a smaller, more localized scale, the verse may be perceived as Mrs. Ma's own confession of her hypocritical character, her double-faced nature.

It is through hypocrisy and duplicity that Mrs. Ma manages to win the complete trust and respect of even those she is most happy to get rid of. That she takes great pains concealing her true color is evidenced in the following episode. Right after her secret tryst with Clerk Chao in which the foul plot is mentioned for the first time, Mrs. Ma is seen putting on her mask again:

> Mrs. Ma: Clerk Chao is gone. I'll put away the poison for the time being and bide my time. <u>Ya</u>! I almost forgot: today is the child's birthday. I'll call for my lord and we'll go to the temples to offer incense and [make donations to] gild the images of Buddha. (<u>Exit.</u>)

> (<u>YCH</u>, p. 1109)

Behold, a Mrs. Ma pious and loving! Such acts as incense-offering and the gilding of Buddhist images on behalf of the child are supposed to bring him good luck and protection. In this case these gestures are calculated to seem twice as noble and unselfish since the child is Hai-t'ang's and not Mrs. Ma's. The playwright loses no time pointing up the success of Mrs. Ma's camouflage. Immediately after the dissembler's exit, Hai-t'ang comes on stage with this piece of monologue:

> It's been five years since I married Lord Ma. . . . The
> child I bore is named Longevity. Ever since his birth--
> even from the time he was in swaddling clothes--he has
> been in the care of my "sister," and he is five now. Today
> is his birthday. My lord and "sister" took him to the
> temples to offer incense and gild the Buddhist images. . . .

(<u>YCH</u>, p. 1109)

One gathers from Hai-t'ang's words that Mrs. Ma's scheme began five years ago and has been going on quite smoothly. There is not the slightest indication that Hai-t'ang suspects anything. One must at least give Mrs. Ma credit for being patient and perseverant--even though hers is a malicious endeavor.

Hai-t'ang, unaware of Mrs. Ma's motivation, is genuinely grateful for what the latter has done for her. In the two arias that follow the monologue just quoted, Hai-t'ang sings of her contentment with life. Since her marriage with Lord Ma, she declares, there are

混江龍 Hun-chiang lung

> No more fear of official summons,
> No more household responsibilities,
> No more patrons coming and going,
> No more bullying from the neighbors,
> No more concerns about family properties:
> There are no more worldly cares.

The general comments are followed up by more specific allusions to the bliss of her marital life with Lord Ma:

> Daily, in great joy, the two of us would exchange
>   our tender thoughts,
> And sleep late till the melting sunshine fell on
>   the screened window.

Then Hai-t'ang acknowledges her indebtedness to the kindness and generosity of Mrs. Ma, her dear "sister":

> For company I have a husband who truly cares;
> In addition I have a sister who shelters me as would
> my own dear mother. . . .

(YCH, p. 1110)

Irony springs from the sharp contrast between Hai-t'ang's naiveté and Mrs. Ma's calculations, and the loyalty of one is a true measure of the adroitness of the other. Here then is one of the places where the delineation of Mrs. Ma through the opinions of others is done.

Years of industrious dissembling on the part of the hypocritical Mrs. Ma have won her the hearts of Lord Ma and Hai-t'ang. But in addition to being patient and dedicated, Mrs. Ma is also shown as being resolute and decisive, capable of exploiting an opportunity as soon as it arises. For her, the long-awaited moment comes when Chang Lin, Hai-t'ang's intemperate brother, returns from a self-inflicted exile and humbly begs for help from his sister whom he once denounced. The following excerpts from Act I offer, in concrete terms, a close look into a shrewd (albeit evil) mind in operation. It is also the act that precipitates Hai-t'ang's misfortune.

Finding the stranger standing by her house to be none other than the elder brother of Hai-t'ang, Mrs. Ma initiates an inquiry:

Mrs. Ma: Uncle, what have you come to see your sister for?

Chang: I tremble to say this but I am so destitute I can hardly survive. So I came to find my sister and ask for some money.

Mrs. Ma: How much did she give you?

Chang: She said you have the sole control over the entire family property and she has no say in it. She gave me not a cent.

Mrs. Ma: Uncle, you're deceived. Since your sister came to our house, she has given birth to an heir, who is now five years old.--He's your nephew!--and now she has control over the entire family fortune. I have no son (she mimes striking her chest) so I have nothing!

As you're brother to Hai-t'ang, I will treat you as
my own brother and go ask your sister to help you. If
I succeed, don't be overjoyed; if I fail, don't feel bitter:
it all depends on your luck. Wait by the gate.

Chang: I understand. What a sensible woman!

(YCH, p. 1111)

Already Mrs. Ma knows how she will proceed. She goes in to confer
with Hai-t'ang and "plead" Chang Lin's case:

Hai-t'ang: But all my clothes and head ornaments were gifts
from you and my lord. What do I have to give him?

Mrs. Ma: The clothes and ornaments were given you: they
are yours. What would be wrong with giving them to
your own brother?

Hai-t'ang: Sister, I'm afraid it is not right to do so. What
could I say if our lord should inquire about them?

Mrs. Ma: Then I'll intercede for you, and we'll get you more.
Quickly take them off and give them to your brother. . . .

(YCH, pp. 1111-12)

After she has thus talked Hai-t'ang into her trap, Mrs. Ma also sees to
it that her own image as a generous person is enhanced. She returns to
Chang Lin with Hai-t'ang's articles and says:

Uncle, because of these things even I feel you're wronged.
Little did I know that your sister could be so heartless. She
has so many clothes and head ornaments but refuses to part
with any for you--as if they were her very flesh and bone!

Now these few pieces are the dowry that my parents gave
me. I give them to you. Uncle, you must not refuse them
simply because they are nearly worthless.

(YCH, p. 1112)

In terms of the interrelationship among the dramatic characters,
Mrs. Ma's distortion serves two purposes. On one hand, it buttresses
Chang Lin's earlier observation that Mrs. Ma is "a sensible woman."
On the other hand, it further reinforces his already bitter resentment
toward his sister Hai-t'ang:

Chang Lin: Sister . . . you're my own sister, born of the
same parents, and yet when I asked for some help, you
gave me nothing! . . . This lady here, a stranger to
me, yet she provides me with clothes and ornaments! . . .

(YCH, p. 1112)

Apparently Mrs. Ma has devised another victory. For Hai-t'ang, however, the most serious damage, the one that really counts, is inflicted
when Mrs. Ma exposes the reason for her actions and accuses her of
infidelity:

Lord Ma: Wife, why are all Hai-t'ang's clothes and ornaments
missing?

Mrs. Ma: Had you not brought it up, my lord, I would find
it difficult to tell you. My lord has doted too much on
her just because she bore you an heir. But neither of
us could have imagined that, behind your back, she has
been supporting a paramour! And she is always indulging
in the impure act!

Today, with you and me out to offer incense, she
gave all her clothes and head ornaments to her adulterer.
She was looking for something to cover herself with when
I, coming home ahead of you, caught her red-handed.
And I forbade her to put on any clothes and ornaments,
so that upon your return you could personally take care
of the matter.

This is not jealousy on my part; she brought it all
on herself.

Lord Ma: So Hai-t'ang gave them all to her lover! I should
have known it!--She was a prostitute before and. . . .
But such disgrace! . . . I shall die of it!

(YCH, p. 1112)

For Mrs. Ma, however, one finishing touch still awaits her
attention: the poisoning of her husband. Murder by poison is conventional stuff to be expected from this type of tsa-chü, yet, even here,
Mrs. Ma appears less than conventional:

[Lord Ma, driven to near apoplexy, has requested a bowl of
hot soup and Mrs. Ma has ordered Hai-t'ang to prepare it.]

(Enter Hai-t'ang with soup.)

Hai-t'ang: Sister, here is the soup.

Mrs. Ma: Bring it here. I'll taste it. (She mimes tasting the soup.) There is not enough salt and it lacks spice. Go get some: be quick!

(Exit Hai-t'ang in obeisance.)

Mrs. Ma: Let me take the poison that I put away the other day and pour it into the soup. (She mimes pouring in the poison.) Hai-t'ang, be quick!

(Reenter Hai-t'ang.)

Hai-t'ang: . . . Sister, here you are.

Mrs. Ma (miming stirring the soup): Hai-t'ang, take it to our lord.

Hai-t'ang: Sister, would you please do it? I'm afraid the sight of me will only aggravate my lord.

Mrs. Ma: But if you don't go, he will believe that you are defying him! (Exit.)

Hai-t'ang: I see. . . .

(YCH, p. 1113-14)

Notice here the playwright has fleshed out the conventional episode and staged a minuscule drama which throws further light on the personalities of both Hai-t'ang and Mrs. Ma: one is meek and easily manipulated, the other always prepared and dominating. Mrs. Ma does not even have to wait for Hai-t'ang's response, confident that the latter will eventually see--and do--things her way.

Another reason for Mrs. Ma's explosive dynamics in the play is that she is a person of action, always looking ahead and seldom dwelling on past accomplishments. Toward the end of Act I she is seen congratulating herself on her recent successes, but only briefly:

See? She's trapped by my scheme. The entire family fortune, along with the child, will soon be mine. (She reconsiders.)

Ha! You'd better think it over: the child is not mine by birth. She'd call as witnesses the two grannies who

delivered the baby and shaved its head, as well as the
neighbors who have watched him grow up. If they don't
testify to my advantage at the court, all my effort would
go down the drain.

Now, the black pupils in human eyes cannot resist
the lure of white silver. I'll simply have to take care of
that. To each and every one of them I'll offer one tael
of silver, and they'll stand by me. . . .

(YCH, p. 1115)

The monologue shows that Mrs. Ma is fully aware not only of her own
weaknesses but of the weaknesses of those she deals with. She has
quick insight into human nature. And she is a doer: in the next moment
she has already done her part and is seen instructing Clerk Chao to
have everything fixed in the yamen, where she anticipates a lawsuit.

These instances, each in its own way, contribute to the portrait
of Mrs. Ma. Their impact on the audience is multiplied because all of
them are packed into the first act. The audience not only grasps the
essential traits of the villainess' personality through her own words,
they also are made familiar with some important details from Lord Ma,
Hai-t'ang, and Chang Lin. The first act of Circle is certainly Mrs. Ma's
act. She continues to dominate in Act II, for although she does not have
an active part there, everything goes exactly as she had planned. Her
influence dwindles in the third act where she suffers her first setback by
failing to have Hai-t'ang murdered; but only in the last act when Judge
Pao has tricked her devious and self-serving lover to confess does Mrs.
Ma acknowledge defeat. Even there, her posture is unexpectedly defiant
though admittedly comical when she declares that "one death is as bad
as another. And when we're dead we can be husband and wife, forever:
what comfort!" (YCH, p. 1129) Characteristically, she is still looking
ahead.

No Ordinary Innkeeper: Hairpins

A frequently encountered figure in Yüan drama is the tien-hsiao-
erh 店小二 . The Chinese term for the owner of any small shop--an
innkeeper or a tavern owner, for example--carries with it an overtone
at once contemptuous and intimate. This epithet in turn defines the role
he generally plays: his presence scarcely offers anything more than
comic relief. Only occasionally does the comedy thus generated bear

significantly on the drama being enacted. One such rare instance we
have seen in Circle: the taverner whose pants' seat is "used for a wine
filter" does contribute to what appears a deliberate effort in the play
toward the scatological or obscene (q.v. p. 65ff.). In most cases (Circle
not excepted), however, the tien-hsiao-erh's function in the drama is
all but negligible. In Chu-sha-tan珠砂擔 (YCH, #23), a play outside
of the judgment reversal group, no less than three innkeepers make
their appearances one after another--because the star of the play, running away from a potential murderer, keeps changing his lodging. The
first innkeeper is given minimal lines, and the other two are only clownish dupes.

In contrast with the slight importance conventionally attached to
the role of a tien-hsiao-erh, the Innkeeper in Hairpins merits special
attention. From the beginning he is closely associated with the ups and
downs of Scholar Chao, star of the play. The Innkeeper joins Chao's
wife and son to form a trio which represents all that is conventional
and mundane, a sharp contrast to the style of the unworldly scholar who
loves to take shelter in the past when it is the present that he has to face
(for a detailed analysis of Scholar Chao's characterization see Chapter II,
p. 46ff.). Together, the three keep importuning the scholar, forcing
him to take occasional excursions out of his comforting realm of impracticality and into the reality of workaday life. As Scholar Chao's fortune
fluctuates, the Innkeeper shares with him in his own way the joy of success and the sorrow of failure. It is also the Innkeeper, not the befud-
dled judges or anyone else close to the judicial system, who on his own
initiative captures the true culprit, rescues Scholar Chao, and restores
justice at the end of the play. Thus, the significance of this Innkeeper's
role is seen not only in his relationship with the other characters, but
even in the direction and structure of the drama. Additionally, the
Innkeeper is portrayed throughout the play in some depth as a sympathetic character. He is often trivial, sometimes mercenary, but always
human.

The play opens with Scholar Chao worried over his financial situation: he owes the Innkeeper rent and does not know what to do. At this
point the trio starts their concerted performance:

Innkeeper (mimes knocking at the door): Open the door!

Mrs. Chao: I'll get it. Brother, what do you want?

Innkeeper: Master scholar, you don't appear to me to be
someone with a promising future. Sister, ask him for

a letter of divorce and marry an official or an influential person or a rich guy. I'll serve as your go-between.

Mrs. Chao: Brother, that's what I have in mind. Chao Ngo, did you hear that? Our brother here wants the bill paid, but what have I got to give him? You just wouldn't go and take the examination. Now, if you become an official, I would be a lady!

Child: Daddy, I'm hungry!

Mrs. Chao: Since you can't support me in any case, give me a divorce.

Innkeeper: Pay the room and board!

(WP, p. 184)

Exactly how serious the Innkeeper and company are is hard to determine. On one hand, all this is made to seem a put-up job. Before the end of the prologue, Scholar Chao does make up his mind to try his luck in the imperial examination, and the Innkeeper is quick to take credit for it: "See? But for our taunting he wouldn't have sat for the exam" (WP, p. 184). On the other hand, the same kind of nagging is repeated at least four times by members of the trio later in the play when Chao fails to bring home any money, and one has reason to suspect that the importuners do mean what they say. The question need not be resolved, since both interpretations are plausible and not necessarily mutually exclusive.

In any event, Chao takes the examination--and finishes first. But the ill-starred scholar simply cannot hold on to his luck. His hope of obtaining an official post is dashed when the emperor reneges on a previous appointment. Empty-handed, Scholar Chao returns home to face an elated Innkeeper:

(Enter Innkeeper carrying wine.)

Innkeeper: I am the innkeeper. I heard Scholar Chao has been assigned to an official post. So I pawned my wife's skirt and bought this bottle of wine, waiting to offer him a cup.

Chao: I'm back.

Innkeeper: Congratulations! You're an official now!

(WP, p. 186)

By the time Scholar Chao has explained his circumstances, the Innkeeper's enthusiasm evaporates and his attitude is changed:

> Innkeeper: I had nothing in my house, so I pawned my wife's
> skirt and bought this bottle of wine to celebrate. Now
> that you don't have a job, what's to be done? Pay your
> rent!

(<u>WP</u>, p. 186)

In much the same vein, the justifiably disappointed wife and child of
the scholar also keep up their attack, demanding divorce and food
respectively.

The obnoxious importuning again rouses him and this time Scholar
Chao decides to sell poems to pay his debts. He has no sooner sold one,
however, than a stranger cries out for help. Chao wavers and hesitates,
but eventually comes to the rescue of the stranger by paying off a bully
with the money he has just earned. Once parted with his cash, the Good
Samaritan finds himself again besieged by the disbelieving trio harping
on the same tune:

> Mrs. Chao: What am I waiting for? I'll marry someone
> else!
>
> Innkeeper: I'll be your go-between.
>
> Child: Daddy, I'm starved to death!

(<u>WP</u>, p. 190)

The Innkeeper furthermore removes the Chaos from their first-class
room to shabby quarters. In Act II alone, such mortifying words or
measures occur three times, and the Innkeeper is always involved in
one way or another.

As luck and Yüan drama would have it, the stranger Scholar Chao
so unselfishly rescues from the hands of the bully turns out to be a high
official dressed in plebeian clothes. As <u>quid pro quo</u> he sends Chao ten
gold phoenix hairpins. When the messenger arrives with them, the
scholar is again being badgered by the trio:

> Innkeeper: Pay the rent this minute!
>
> Mrs. Chao: Write me the bill of divorcement!

Innkeeper: Sister, demand the divorce from him and marry
    someone else. I'll serve as your matchmaker.

Child: I want a cake!

Mrs. Chao: Write the divorce now!

Chao: I'll do it when daybreak comes. . . .

(<u>WP</u>, p. 193)

The gift could not have come at a more opportune moment. The situation again drastically reversed, Scholar Chao is in command, if only for a short while. He summons the Innkeeper back:

Innkeeper: Dear brother, what is your wish?

Chao: The official just gave me ten gold hairpins in return.
    I'll give you one as payment in kind.

Innkeeper: I <u>knew</u> you weren't a pauper. I'll clean up the
    first-class room for you to rest. Let me make some
    tea for you. You may move in afterwards. . . .

(<u>WP</u>, p. 193)

As the scholar realizes, this is the way of the world. In the words characteristic of his bookish cant, "It always takes worldly wealth/To achieve things unworldly" (<u>WP</u>, p. 194, 賀新郎 <u>Ho hsin-lang</u>).

The Innkeeper not only quickly adjusts himself to his now well-off tenant, he also makes sure that Mrs. Chao does the same to her husband, as the ensuing scene shows:

Innkeeper: Sister, our dear brother hasn't had anything all
    day. I'll fix some tea and meal for our dear brother.

Mrs. Chao: That's a good idea.

(<u>Exit innkeeper in a hurry. He reenters with meal.</u>)

Innkeeper: Sister, the meal is ready. Entreat our dear
    brother to have some.

Mrs. Chao: Much obliged, dear brother.

Innkeeper: Don't mention it. We're just one happy family.
    Sister, <u>you</u> take the meal to our dear brother, to show
    your respect.

Mrs. Chao: Yes, I will. (She takes the meal to her husband.)

Chao: Dear wife, what is this all about?

Mrs. Chao: I saw you hadn't had anything to eat, so I asked brother innkeeper to make you some food. Do have some.

Innkeeper: Yes, dear brother, do have some.

(WP, p. 194)

The minuscule comedy reveals the petty Innkeeper at his most devious. With cunning and skill he enlists the help of Mrs. Chao in his own efforts to gain the good graces of his tenant. Note especially how he consistently addresses the scholar now as "dear brother" or "our dear brother" (ko-ko 哥哥) as opposed to the former "scholar" (hsiu-ts'ai 秀才). His use of the phrase coincides, of course, with the advent of Chao's new fortune. It first appeared in the previous scene ("Dear brother, what is your wish?" the Innkeeper asked) and has since been habitual with him. In the above quotation the phrase pops up with such regularity and insistence that it rings with an almost sarcastic and certainly comical overtone. Mrs. Chao and the Innkeeper--the latter in particular-- may be justly faulted for being mercenary, but in their self-seeking also lies their humanness. After all, what does one expect of a small innkeeper whose tenant has failed to pay up for months? Or of a wife, for that matter, who has all along been on the verge of starvation? Their weaknesses as human beings are precisely their strength as dramatic characters.

In addition to being an all-too-human comic figure, the Innkeeper plays a key role in the structural development of the drama as well. That his less-than-amiable manner as bill-collector helps plant the impractical scholar more firmly on the ground should be apparent from the foregoing paragraphs. His part in the dénouement proves crucial to the fate of Scholar Chao. Unlike the other judgment reversal plays, where the good judge is frequently endowed with unusual powers (symbolized by imperial emblems such as a golden badge or a sword of authority or both) and exceptional resourcefulness (with which he outsmarts the villain and uncovers the truth), Hairpins features a justice helpless and pathetic. The absence of the conventional duel of wit (between the judge and the villain), in which the good always prevails, creates an impasse in the development of the play: should the innocent scholar be executed as demanded by the first judge who seems to have conclusive evidence against the accused? The circumstance enables the Innkeeper to make his contribution to the course of the play in his own unspectacular way.

It is unspectacular because it is accidental and lacks the kind of theatricality some other trick (like a ghost scene) would provide. What happens to the Innkeeper--for he does not particularly bargain for it--is simply the following: Tiger Li, the murderer who earlier exchanged the stolen silver spoons (now held as evidence against the poor scholar!) for Chao's nine gold hairpins, has taken them to a silversmith to trade for cash. The Innkeeper, himself also hard up, brings his lone hairpin to the same silversmith. A series of events ensues:

Silversmith (examining the Innkeeper's hairpin): I have nine hairpins that are identical with yours.

Innkeeper: You do? Could I have a look?

Silversmith: Certainly. See? Aren't they identical?

Innkeeper: Yes indeed! And because of these nine gold hairpins the life of an innocent man is soon to be lost! Where did you get these?

Silversmith: Brother, they're not mine. Someone came just now and wanted to exchange for cash. He hasn't got the money yet and will soon be back.

Innkeeper: When this guy returns, we'll capture him and save Scholar Chao. Do as I tell you, or I'll hold you responsible!

Silversmith: What does it have to do with me? When he comes we'll arrest him. He should be coming any minute. Hide yourself now.

(Enter Tiger Li.)

Li: Now I'll get my money for the hairpins. Hey, Silversmith, pay me the money for the hairpins.

Innkeeper and Silversmith (capturing Tiger Li): Well, well. So you stole the hairpins. And you would have an innocent person die for you! Come, everybody, take this one and tie him up. We'll go and rescue Scholar Chao.

(WP, p. 200)

Predictably, they arrive at the execution ground just in time, the beheading of Scholar Chao having been delayed because the two confused judges simply cannot reach agreement on a case that neither truly understands. With the missing links now supplied by the Innkeeper, the second judge is ready to proclaim poetic justice as the play draws to its mandatory happy end.

True, the play does not end with a bang but neither does it end
with a whimper. If nothing else, the finale presents the Innkeeper at
his most courageous. Out of indignation and simple humanity, he takes
the initiative--when the opportunity comes his way--to restore justice,
presumably at his own peril. The Innkeeper as plebeian semihero in
this incident and the Innkeeper as a constant pest in previous scenes are
poles apart. The wide spectrum of his potentials is indicative of the
success and vitality of the character portrayal. In all fairness one must
conclude that the humble Innkeeper has a prime role in shaping the
drama; he is the most unconventional innkeeper of the courtroom plays.

Kao Shan: the "Born Loser" in Doll

The preceding sections demonstrated that even a supporting role
in any given play can loom large and become, in a way, the focal point
of interest in the drama--particularly when he has many lines and is
very much talked about; or makes his presence keenly, sometimes pain-
fully and tediously, felt; or both. Kao Shan, the peddler in The Mo-ho-
lo Doll, has none of these attributes. He is a truly "minor" character
in the sense that during the entire course of the play he shows up only
three times (the two consecutive appearances at the beginning of Act II
counted as one), and each time only briefly. Nevertheless, his is an
important role in the drama. In Act I, he allows himself, albeit reluc-
tantly, to break what he insists is a lifelong vow--which is actually
another convention seen in other plays as well--and becomes messenger
for the ailing Li Te-ch'ang. The next act sees him faithfully delivering
the message to Li's wife--but not before he has inadvertently transmitted
the same to Li's cousin, the would-be murderer. Kao Shan finally
reappears, in the last act, as a court witness; and it is with the clue he
provides that the review judge is able to solve the murder case. Thus,
especially with regard to the development of the dramatic plot, Kao
Shan's position in Doll is assuredly unique and most indispensible.

Of greater interest, perhaps, than his function in the plot is the
economy and precision with which Kao Shan's character is drawn. In
limited time and space, he comes vividly alive as an individual with
distinctly recognizable features. Essentially, Kao Shan appears as a
man with a quick tongue but is a born loser. There are moments when
this rustic with his wit and gift of phrase compares well with the Shake-
spearean fool. Although everything he does he does with good intention,
nothing he touches ever comes out exactly right. These two attributes
introduce ingredients of humor, mirth, and warm sympathy. Kao Shan

must have been a crowd-pleaser: he could easily seize--and hold--the attention of his audience.

Let us start with Kao's first encounter (immediately after his debut) with Li Te-ch'ang in the half-ruined temple where both have come for shelter from the pouring rain. Te-ch'ang, taken ill, alone, and fearing for his life, is heartened when he hears someone coming. (In what follows I have made liberal use of Professor Crump's graceful rendition of <u>Doll</u>.)[27]

(Te-ch'ang moves softly across stage and bows.)

Te-ch'ang: Greetings, old one.

Kao (terrified): Gods help me! A ghost!

Te-ch'ang: I am no ghost, I'm a man.

Kao: If you're a man, you shouldn't startle people like that! Call out so a man can tell you're human. But sneaking over and giving greetings right in my ear--in this old temple--with no one about. . . . well, you're lucky it was me, anyone else would have been scared to death!

(Kao reaches down and picks up a pinch of mud.)

Te-ch'ang: What are you doing?

Kao: You scared me so bad my fontanel has opened up.*

(YCH, p. 1371)[28]

An element of the humorous creeps in when attention is unobtrusively called to the inconsistency in Kao's reaction--"you're lucky it was me, anyone else would have been scared to death!" and "you scared me so bad my fontanel has opened up." Already, Kao has been established as a mildly comic character.[29]

Te-ch'ang, who finds out that Kao is bound for his hometown, entreats the latter to take a message for him. The request is at first

---

* "There was a belief that when a young child was badly frightened his fontanel opened up and could be ritually plugged by sticking a daub of mud atop it."--Crump's note.

indirectly declined as Kao declares: "Good brother, there are three
things I've forbidden myself to do all my life: one, to be a go-between
for anyone; two, go security for anyone; and three, to deliver anyone's
message!" (YCH, p. 1371)[30] Though a crystallization of worldly wisdom, Kao's initial response seems tinged with unconcern. But such an
impression is soon removed:

> Te-ch'ang: Look, I'm from the Vinegar Worker's alley in
> Ho-nan Fu, my family name is Li and I am called Te-
> ch'ang. There are three of us in my family, my wife
> Yü-niang, my son Fo-liu and myself. I went to Nan-
> ch'ang to sell and I've come back with a hundred-fold
> profit. . . .
>
> Kao: Stop, stop, stop! (He goes out the door to look; shouts.)
> All of you who've come in out of the rain, let's get to-
> gether and talk a while! What, nobody here? (Comes
> back in door and looks at Te-ch'ang.) Now how about the
> likes of you! Nobody asked you a thing and you begin
> babbling. If there'd been anyone in the place to hear
> you they could have robbed and killed you in a trice.
> Then where would your sales trips have got you? You
> don't even know what kind of man I am. You know what
> they say: "Drawing a tiger you draw the skin; to draw
> the bones is the hardest part. When you know a man you
> know the face, who has ever known a heart?"

$$\text{(YCH, p. 1371)}^{31}$$

Kao Shan's reaction in this connection is characteristic of someone who
has seen enough of the world to be on guard against it, but it marks
him also as a trustworthy person, honest and compassionate: there is
yet hope for Te-ch'ang. And, to the surprise of no one, the interlude
closes with Kao giving in to Te-ch'ang's pleading:

> Te-ch'ang: My only hope was that you would take a message
> to my wife to tell her to come nurse me. If you won't
> deliver the message and I die, it will have been because
> you tampered with my destiny!
>
> Kao: You crafty beggar, you certainly can lay traps. All
> right, I'm breaking a lifelong vow but I'll deliver your
> message. Where do you live, what does [your] store

look like and who are your neighbors? Tell me, then
go rest. . . .

(<u>YCH</u>, p. 1371)[32]

While these words might relieve the audience's anxiety over Li Te-
ch'ang's plight, the born loser has already suffered his first defeat.
For much as Kao Shan's homely wisdom makes him steer clear of another's affairs, he ends up getting crucially involved all the same.
Notice, however, that even in defeat, Kao does not lose his good nature
or sense of humor ("You crafty beggar, you certainly can lay traps,"
and so on)--a characteristic that we continue to discern in the peddler
in subsequent encounters with him.

With his next appearance, Kao Shan brings some misgiving and
more laughter. The misgiving comes with a stroke of irony:

<u>(Enter Kao Shan.)</u>

Kao: I am old Kao Shan finally arrived in Honan city, but I
wonder where Vinegar Alley is? Let me put down my
hampers and enquire of someone. (Sees <u>Li Wen-tao
[Te-ch'ang's cousin and murderer-to-be]</u>) Brother,
could I trouble you to tell me where Vinegar Alley can
be found?

Wen-tao: Why do you ask?

Kao: Well, a certain Li Te-ch'ang lives there. He went
to Nan-ch'ang to sell his wares, returned a hundred
times richer and is now in the Temple of the Guardian
General south of the city quite ill. He asked me to
carry a message for him.

Wen-tao (<u>aside</u>): Things <u>are</u> improving! . . .

(<u>YCH</u>, p. 1372)[33]

Having known what a malicious and unscrupulous person Wen-tao is,
the audience knows what to expect from him. That the canny Kao Shan,
who once admonished Te-ch'ang for not being discreet enough, should
be so offguard and tell a total stranger about Te-ch'ang's newly acquired
fortune, is just one of the ironic twists in the play. (One recalls, for
instance, that Te-ch'ang journeyed all the way to Nan-ch'ang expressly
for the purpose of avoiding a prophesied doom to no avail.) It also

shows how things <u>could</u> go wrong in the hands of the well-meaning peddler.

But the incident is then deliberately touched with comedy, to wit:

> Wen-tao (<u>turns</u>): Old one, where you are now is little Vinegar Alley but there's another called Big Vinegar Alley and to get there you head east and then walk westward until you are facing south. Then go north. When you've gone around a corner you'll see a great sophora tree in front of a gate and a large house with a red-painted door and green-painted windows. Above the door you'll see a bamboo screen and under the screen will be a little tyke of a dog fast asleep--that will be Li Te-ch'ang's house.
>
> Kao: Thank you, brother. (<u>Shoulders his burden and goes muttering.</u>) All right, he said go east and walk west; face south and go north, turn corner, big sophora tree, great house, red door, green windows, bamboo screen and underneath a little tyke sleeping--but suppose that dog should wake up and leave--?
>
> (<u>YCH</u>, p. 1372)[34]

It is quite clear that the "directions" given by Wen-tao are nothing more than a charade meant to muddle the messenger and thereby stall his mission. The episode therefore reaches the height of absurdity when Kao Shan takes the dissembler's words seriously and raises a question perfectly legitimate and logical (under the circumstances)--but totally beside the point. Thus on one hand is rationality and dead earnestness; on the other, calculated misdirection and frivolity. The result of such juxtaposition is comedy that climaxes when the naive peddler returns with his hard-won discovery:

> Kao: I've walked myself to death! I could take that whoreson and . . . he said there was a Big Vinegar Alley but there is no such thing! (<u>Puts down his hampers.</u>) I could take that jackass-begotten, ugly whoreson . . . ! <u>This</u> is Vinegar Alley and he sent me right around the city! And all that time it was here!
>
> (<u>YCH</u>, pp. 1372-73)[35]

With Kao Shan, one piece of bad luck seems to beget another.
Even as he is standing right in front of Te-ch'ang's shop, the destina-
tion of his message, Kao's lot is not much improved:

([Te-ch'ang's wife] Yü-niang comes out the door and sees
[Kao Shan].)

Yü-niang: See here old man, don't you know any better than
to stand in the doorway of a shop that's trying to do business. What are you doing there anyway?

Kao: Now we know my entire fate! I am doomed to be walked
to death by a whoreson or talked to death by a woman!
Kao Shan, you've no one to blame but yourself for this!
Had you refused to deliver Li Te-ch'ang's message it
would never have happened!

Yü-niang: Old one! Where did you see Li Te-ch'ang? Please,
come in and have a cup of tea!

Kao [sarcastically]: What? And interfere with business!

(YCH, p. 1373)[36]

After all that has happened to him, it is an appealing anticlimax that the
peddler should now come to the realization that Lady Luck has not been
with him. His complaints are justified and one can genuinely sympathize
with him, but Kao Shan obviously has no use for other people's sympathy.
The good old man is made of such stuff as to rebound easily from disappointment and exasperation. The next moment, he is his old self again:
a bit sarcastic maybe, but still good-natured, likeable, and compassionate. The important message delivered, the interlude ends on a
happy and heartwarming note:

Child: Mama, I want one of those Mo-ho-lo dolls.

Yü-niang (slaps child): You stupid child! We've hardly
enough for food, where would we get the money for
that?

Kao: Don't scold the child. I'll give him a Mo-ho-lo.
Take good care of it now, son, don't break it playing
with it. Look, here on the bottom--my name. It
says, "made by Kao Shan." And when your father
comes home and sees it he'll have proof that I delivered his message. (Exit.)

(YCH, p. 1373)[37]

And a proof the doll does become--not for the hapless Te-ch'ang but for the review judge. Again Kao Shan, against his inclination, involves himself further in the murder case. The following interrogation scene from the final act displays the peddler's rustic wit at its best:

> Chang Ting: Before you saw Liu Yü-niang did you do anything else?
>
> Kao: Oh, now I remember! When I reached the city wall I took a good leak.
>
> Chang Ting: Nobody asked you about that!
>
> Kao: Well, when I got into the city I asked directions of a shopkeeper and in front of his place was a torture shell.
>
> Chang Ting: You mean a tortoise-shell.
>
> Kao: I guess I know when something was a torture. And beside the door stood this mortal pester--
>
> Chang Ting: You mean mortar and pestle.
>
> Kao: Maybe I do, but what he did was pester me to death. Anyway, inside the place there sat this veterinarian--
>
> Chang Ting: You mean physician.
>
> Kao: No, horse doctor!
>
> Chang Ting: How could you tell that?
>
> Kao: He could never have played such jackass tricks if he hadn't been. Anyway, he called himself "Second Physician of Lu". . . .

> (YCH, pp. 1386-87)[38]

It is a jeu d'ésprit, the flavor of which is admirably preserved in Professor Crump's translation. By reminiscing about the Second Physician of Lu, Kao Shan has rendered the court (again by accident) an invaluable service. His reward? To wit:

> Chang Ting: Chang Ch'ien, give Kao Shan eighty strokes because he shouldn't have made the Mo-ho-lo.
>
> Chang Ch'ien (pantomimes flogging): Sixty, seventy, eighty-- out you go!
>
> Kao: What was that for?

Chang Ch'ien: For making a Mo-ho-lo.

(YCH, p. 1386)[39]

The treatment Kao Shan receives in the last scene seems hardly justifiable and would suggest the playwright's catering to the somewhat bloodthirsty taste of his audience. The speculation is buttressed by the fact that, earlier, Chang Ting ordered his man to "flog [Kao Shan] all the way from here to the yamen" and Kao complained, upon arrival, that "I've done nothing to make this clown beat me like he was paddling a boat upstream!" (YCH, p. 1384)[40] On the other hand, there is no denying that this is a marvelous finishing touch to the portrait of a born loser. The playwright must have found it hard not to drive home such an image: consistency and harmony in the sketch of Kao Shan is achieved at the expense of presenting Chang Ting--the upright judge of the review trial--as arbitrary and whimsical. Similarly, the half-joking, half-complaining retort of Kao Shan--

Eighty strokes for a Mo-ho-lo--I bet I'd have lost my head if I'd made an Indra!

(YCH, p. 1386)[41]

does not come as a surprise; rather, it is in character with the style of the wry and quick-witted peddler. All things considered, the playwright must be credited with the creation of a comic character who is functional, consistent, appealing and warm. Particularly in view of the economy and precision with which this is accomplished, the portrait of Kao Shan may be considered a miniature masterpiece.

IV. POSTSCRIPTS

Structure and Theme

In a study which sets out to explore the artistic "wholes" of a group of dramas, the conspicuous absence of discourses on structure and theme calls for explanation. On the surface at least, the neglect of structure appears to be justified. Dramatic structure per se did not enter our discussion because the seven plays were selected precisely for their structural similarity. Once that was settled, little could be gained from further pursuit of that topic whereas exploration in the areas of language and character manipulation would bear fruit. All seven plays are courtroom dramas featuring first a miscarriage of justice and then a redress of the injustice. In most cases the climax is reached in the second act, with the foul deed accomplished and the innocent scapegoat trapped; in others, all this is highlighted in the third act. Unraveling of plot routinely comes in the fourth and last act when villainy is exposed (or tricked) and justice restored.

In other words, the dramatic events of the judgment reversal plays take place in a certain fixed sequence. Introduction, murder in cold blood, false allegation, and courtroom scenes (complete with physical torture and subsequent "confessions") make up the first half of the dramatic action. The second half comprises the arrival of a reformer acting as review judge, a new trial (with still more torture and confession), gathering of evidence and a few tricks by the second judge, and, finally, the restoration of order and justice. Limiting as the rigid convention is, individual playwrights still managed to work in some of their own inventions--but only in unobtrusive ways. For instance, whereas in most plays the review judge is solely responsible for uncovering the truth, in others (such as Hairpins and Doll) certain seemingly insignificant characters prove to be even more important for the dénouement. The basic structure, however, remains unchanged.

147

148

The dramatic structure carries thematic implications. Crime and punishment, law and order, justice (or injustice), corrupt officialdom, reward of the virtuous--such terms readily come to mind when one reflects on the central ideas the judgment reversal dramas appear to embody. As a matter of fact, the implicit presence of these ideas has made the Yüan courtroom plays darlings of critics of a particularly strong "socialistic" bent.

Nonetheless, it is also possible to locate the playwright's message on a more philosophical plane. Instead of--or in addition to--criticizing this or that individual official and condemning this or that political system, he is perhaps ridiculing life itself, mocking the futility of human endeavors. Again the dramatic structure provides the clue. The accidental and offhand manner in which "justice" is brought about at each play's end strongly suggests that justice as human beings understand the term is elusive or possibly unattainable. Man may (and indeed should) struggle for justice: the review trial--the ultimate convention in these dramas--implies as much. Yet man can achieve it only through dubious means. He relies on supernatural intervention (ghosts and accidents) and resorts to measures that are themselves a mockery of justice (extortions and tricks). In short, although the appearance of restored harmony and order at curtain time may be real on a certain level, beneath it one always perceives something profoundly pessimistic, perhaps even tragic.

Summary

The Yüan tsa-chü is a unique phenomenon in the long history of Chinese literature. No sooner had it come into existence as full-fledged theater than it flourished, reached its peak, and declined--all in the latter half of the thirteenth century. With the passage of time, Yüan drama as a performing art has suffered irredeemable losses. Today, there is no hope of ever recovering the music which must have been largely responsible for the genre's immense popularity in the Yüan dynasty playhouse. Historical documents being scandalously sparse, even evidence on the theatrical arts has to be culled mainly from the extant play texts, which were perhaps the least revered (hence the most tampered with) form of literature of their day. Of the seven hundred odd plays we know existed, less than a quarter have survived. To make things worse, later scholars and critics had a share in muddling and distorting the picture. Misconceptions such as the "poetic fallacy" and the "socialistic" cult have discovered both less and more, respectively, than was dreamed of by the Yüan tsa-chü author.

Yet the cause is not entirely lost. Scholarly efforts in recent years have been especially encouraging. For instance, although we may have lost tsa-chü's music for good, we can still hope to learn more about its musicology, thanks to modern students of the genre who are too optimistic to give up.[1] The theatrical aspects--costumes, performing modes, player's art, and so on--have also intrigued noted scholars in the last decade or two.[2] Last but not least, these Yüan plays can still be enjoyed and fruitfully studied as dramatic literature, as I hope the present volume and other critical works have proved.[3] If these efforts grow and bear fruit, a more complete and gratifying picture of the Yüan theater will certainly emerge.

One need not defend Yüan drama's seeming lack of sophistication, either. First, as has been noted elsewhere in this study, the music of the tsa-chü must have been extremely sophisticated: it is simply our misfortune that it has not come down to us. Secondly, a modern reader's demand for more subtlety of characterization and structure is certainly anachronistic: after all, it was in the thirteenth century when tsa-chü suddenly erupted, as if from nowhere, to give China its first well-defined dramatic form. Let the reader compare these Yüan scripts with European dramas of the same century.

Critics and scholars in the field of Yüan tsa-chü today need to be equipped with only one thing: an open mind, a mind open to receive the tsa-chü as drama, and to listen with discrimination to the extant texts.

SCENARIOS OF THE JUDGMENT REVERSAL PLAYS

1. "The Child Shen-nu-erh," YCH, #33, pp. 557-76.

Act I

At the insistence of his wife La-mei, Li Te-yi entreats his brother, Te-jen, to split the Li family inheritance. The proposition is met with Te-jen's strong rejection. Again instigated by his wife, Te-yi comes up with a "compromise": that Te-yi should divorce his wife, A-Ch'en. To this Te-jen finally consents, but he is so exasperated that he dies of anger before signing the divorce document. A-Ch'en and Shen-nu-erh, her child by Te-jen, survive.

Wedge

One day the yüan-kung 院公 , an elderly servant of the Li's, takes Shen-nu-erh out to play in the streets. While the child is left unattended by the bridge, a drunken Li Te-yi happens by and, recognizing his nephew, takes him home. Ho Cheng, a yamen functionary, witnesses the incident.

Act II

La-mei takes advantage of her husband's drunkenness and murders Shen-nu-erh by strangling him. Waking up to find the child dead, Te-yi must take his orders from La-mei, who threatens to implicate him if he does not. Together, they bury the child in the drainage ditch. Meanwhile, the yüan-kung is looking everywhere for Shen-nu-erh, in vain. Tired, he falls asleep, and the child appears in his dream to narrate the horrible deed. The startled servant wakes up and reports to the child's mother, A-Ch'en.

Act III

After a search to no avail, A-Ch'en and the yüan-kung are instead named murderers and dragged to court. Clerk Sung, who takes a bribe from Te-yi, gives A-Ch'en a severe flogging and succeeds in extracting a "confession" from her.

Act IV

Judge Pao arrives to review the case. He suspects a miscarriage of justice but knows not how to proceed. Ho Cheng, who earlier witnessed the incident at the bridge, relates what he saw. Li Te-yi is arrested, but La-mei remains adamant and denies having anything to do with the case. The ghost of Shen-nu-erh is invited into the courtroom to recount the deed, and the villains are sentenced and justice restored.

2. "Judgment on the Kerchief," YCH, #39, pp. 668-86.

Act I

Wang Hsiao-erh, a pauper, is begging by the residence of the wealthy Liu family when he hits and breaks a commode by mistake. A heated quarrel ensues. Demeaned in public, Wang threatens to kill Liu if they should "meet in the back alley." Thereupon Mrs. Liu demands from Wang a "warranty of life" whereby Wang would be held responsible for anything that might happen to her husband in a period of one hundred days.

Wedge

Mrs. Liu summons her paramour, Monk Wang, and gives him orders to get rid of her husband, which the monk does by slaying him. Wang Hsiao-erh, however, gets the blame.

Act II

Tortured beyond endurance, Wang Hsiao-erh not only admits to the charges but fabricates a location where he supposedly hid two pieces of evidence--a ring and a kerchief. A country cousin who has come to collect payment for straw is in the prison cell and witnessed the beating.

Once out of the cell, the straw seller runs into Monk Wang and describes to him what he saw in the prison. Subsequently the monk places the "loot" to accord with Wang Hsiao-erh's "confession." Chang Ch'ien, a court attendant ordered to go and fetch the two pieces of evidence, also happens by the monk on his mission.

With everything against him, Wang Hsiao-erh is scheduled to be executed when Chang Ting, the chief clerk, intervenes, declaring the evidence insufficient. The judge/prefect gives him three days to discover the truth.

Act III

Chang Ting interrogates Wang Hsiao-erh and the straw seller. An accidental remark of the latter reminds Chang Ch'ien of his chance meeting with the monk. Pursuing the lead, Chang Ting then tricks Mrs. Liu into revealing the identity of Monk Wang and the illicit lovers confess to their crime.

Act IV

Cleared of any guilt, Wang Hsiao-erh is set free. Chang Ting is rewarded by the prefect for the successful investigation; the corrupt clerk, stripped of his title now, is exiled.

3. "Rescue of a Filial Son," YCH, #44, pp. 756-76.

Act I

Wang Hsiao-jan, Prefect of Ta-hsing, arrives at a village on a conscription mission. Yang Hsieh-tsu, the younger son of Mrs. Yang, a widow, longs to join the military but his mother insists that Hsing-tsu, his elder brother, be conscripted. Mrs. Yang's insistence leads Prefect Wang to suspect that Hsing-tsu is probably a stepson. After inquiry, however, he discovers to his surprise that the reverse is true and that the widow is in fact doing everything to shield Hsieh-tsu.

Before departure, Hsing-tsu leaves his wife Ch'un-hsiang a sword as a gift for her brother.

Wedge

A half year later, Ch'un-hsiang is sent for by her own mother. Mrs. Yang orders Hsieh-tsu to escort his sister-in-law through most of the journey. Once they are separated, a herbal doctor comes along

and orders Ch'un-hsiang to deliver a baby for a woman he has earlier
abducted. When the woman dies, the doctor kidnaps Ch'un-hsiang,
accusing her of killing the woman with the sword.

Act II

Ch'un-hsiang's mother comes to the Yangs and discovers that her
daughter has been gone for half a month. A search follows and it produces only a sword and a woman's corpse decomposed beyond recogni-
tion. Ch'un-hsiang's mother suspects that Hsieh-tsu foully murdered
her daughter after unsuccessful advances. When the case is brought to
court, the clerk in charge bullies and threatens, but Mrs. Yang remains
unintimidated and refuses to acknowledge the corpse as her daughter-
in-law's.

Act III

Physical torture compels Yang Hsieh-tsu to admit to the murder
charge. Disregarding Mrs. Yang's insistence on making an autopsy
first, the clerk goes on to prosecute her son.

Act IV

By accident, Ch'un-hsiang is reunited with her husband, Hsing-
tsu, who has returned from the battlefield an honored officer. Meanwhile, Hsieh-tsu is having a hard time defending himself against the
evidence of the sword. The timely arrival of Hsing-tsu and Ch'un-hsiang
saves the younger brother from the headsman's axe.

4. "The Chalk Circle," YCH, #64, pp. 1107-29.

Wedge

Chang Lin, ashamed of his sister Hai-t'ang's profession as a
courtesan, leaves home after quarreling with her. Later, after some
bargaining, Hai-t'ang's "mother" consents to marrying Hai-t'ang to the
wealthy Lord Ma.

Act I

Mrs. Ma receives from Clerk Chao, her paramour, some poison
meant to take her husband's life. It being the fifth birthday of Hai-t'ang's
child, the Mas are out visiting temples to offer donations.

Chang Lin returns home a beggar, asking for the mercy of his now prosperous sister. Still sour over their previous disputes and also fearing gossip, Hai-t'ang refuses to help her brother. Mrs. Ma comes along and presuades her to give all her clothes and ornaments to Chang Lin, promising to intercede for Hai-t'ang should Lord Ma ever raise any questions. Chang Lin, convinced that the gifts are from Mrs. Ma, leaves still with a grudge against his sister.

The suspicious Lord Ma does raise questions, and all Mrs. Ma does is to fabricate a story about Hai-t'ang and her "secret lover." Taken in by his wife, Lord Ma gives Hai-t'ang a sound beating and then falls ill. Mrs. Ma manages to put the poison in the soup Hai-t'ang prepares for Lord Ma, and when the latter dies, she accuses Hai-t'ang of murder.

Act II

"Soft Su," the prefect in charge, delegates his power to Clerk Chao (Mrs. Ma's paramour). With the help of the witnesses whom Mrs. Ma has bribed, Chao is able to declare Hai-t'ang guilty of the charge, to which Hai-t'ang, under torture, is forced to admit. It is also determined that Hai-t'ang has tried to steal the child from the true mother, Mrs. Ma.

Act III

Hai-t'ang is dispatched to K'ai-feng to be sentenced. On the way she meets her brother, now a foreman in the K'ai-feng court. The two are reconciled after Hai-t'ang tells her version of the story. Meanwhile, to make sure that Hai-t'ang is murdered on the road, Mrs. Ma and Clerk Chao have followed and overtaken them. Chang Lin tries to capture them without success.

Act IV

In the K'ai-feng court, Judge Pao draws a chalk circle in which the child is placed. Mrs. Ma and Hai-t'ang are asked to pull the child out: she who succeeds in doing so shall be recognized as the true mother. After Hai-t'ang gives up twice, Judge Pao gets her to say why: she was afraid the child might get hurt should she also attempt to pull on him as Mrs. Ma did. Thereupon Judge Pao gives the child to Hai-t'ang. The murder case is drawn to a conclusion when Clerk Chao is summoned and forced to confess.

5. "The Mo-ho-lo Doll," YCH, #79, pp. 1368-88.

Wedge

Li Te-ch'ang departs for Nan-ch'ang to avoid a predicted disaster, leaving Yü-niang, his wife, to take care of the dry goods shop and their child, Fo-liu.

Act I

Te-ch'ang's cousin, Li Wen-tao, takes advantage of his absence and makes frequent advances to Yü-niang but is each time rejected.

Returning with a hundredfold profit, Te-ch'ang is drenched in a rainstorm. He takes shelter in an abandoned old temple outside of his hometown. Suffering from a severe chill, he entreats Kao Shan, a peddler who has also come into the temple to keep out of the rain, to take a message for him. After some hesitation, Kao agrees.

Act II

Once in town, Kao Shan asks for direction from Wen-tao (the would-be adulterer). Wen-tao tricks the message from the peddler and sends him off in the wrong direction. Kao finally meets Yü-niang and delivers the message. He also leaves Fo-liu a Mo-ho-lo doll as a gift.

In the meantime, Wen-tao goes to the temple, poisons his cousin, and takes all his money. By the time Yü-niang gets Te-ch'ang back home, he is already a dead man.

Wen-tao drags Yü-niang to court for murdering Te-ch'ang. The bribed court clerk finds Yü-niang guilty as charged and has her beaten until she agrees to confess.

Act III

A new prefect assumes office and is about to have Yü-niang decapitated when Clerk Chang Ting, returning from a mission, intercedes, declaring a mistrial. Offended, the new prefect gives Chang Ting three days to come up with a perfect solution to the case.

Act IV

The Mo-ho-lo doll leads Chang Ting to Kao Shan, who recalls his encounter with Wen-tao on the day he delivered the message. The case comes to light when Wen-tao's father is tricked by Chang Ting to name his own son as the murderer.

6. "Injustice to Tou Ngo," YCH, #86, pp. 1499-1517.

Wedge

Unable to pay back a debt of forty taels of silver, Tou T'ien-chang solves his problem by selling his daughter, the seven-year-old Tuan-yün, to Granny Ts'ai, to become the latter's daughter-in-law eventually. T'ien-chang himself then leaves for the capital to seek his fortune.

Act I

Thirteen years later, Tuan-yün, who is called Tou Ngo now, is a youthful widow whose husband has been dead for two years. One day, Granny Ts'ai is out collecting a debt from Doctor Lu and the latter attempts to murder her. Two bums, Old Chang and his son, Donkey Chang, happen by and save Granny Ts'ai. In return, they seek the hands of Granny Ts'ai and Tou Ngo in marriage. The old woman consents under pressure, but her daughter-in-law is strongly opposed to the proposal. The Changs have to bide their time.

Act II

Donkey Chang manages to get poison from Doctor Lu. When Granny Ts'ai falls ill, he puts the poison in her soup, which she offers to Old Chang. As a result, Old Chang, instead of Granny Ts'ai, is killed. Donkey Chang holds Tou Ngo responsible for his father's death, for it is she who prepared the soup. They go to court.

There, not even the severest torture can bend Tou Ngo's spirit; but when the judge threatens to torture her mother-in-law, Tou Ngo changes her mind and confesses to the false charge.

Act III

Before execution, Tou Ngo makes known three last wishes: first, that her blood, instead of dripping on the ground, might fly up to stain the white cloth banner hanging from a spear; second, that snow might fall (even though it is summer!) to cover up her body; and third, that a drought might plague the area for three years--all to remind people of the injustice done to her. Much to the astonishment of the officials, no sooner has Tou Ngo been beheaded than her first two wishes are fulfilled.

Act IV

Tou T'ien-chang, now an imperial inspector, has come to Ch'u-chou, a place in drought for three years now. His daughter, Tou Ngo, appears in his dream to tell her sad story. Next day, the ghost of Tou Ngo reappears in court and, with Doctor Lu as witness, Tou T'ien-chang is able to pin down the true culprit and restore his daughter's name·posthumously.

7. "The Gold Phoenix Hairpins," WP, #113, pp. 184-201.

Wedge

Chao Ngo, a poor scholar, cannot pay his rent. Importuned by a trio made up of his wife, his child, and the Innkeeper his landlord, the scholar decides to try his luck at the imperial examination.

Act I

Although he comes out of the examination in first-place, an unfortunate mistake in etiquette costs him a promised position. He returns home empty-handed, much to the disappointment of his family and his landlord. His wife, encouraged by the Innkeeper, again threatens to divorce him. Chao says he will try his luck this time by selling poems.

Act II

The scholar has just sold his first poem for two hundred coppers when Tiger Li, a bully, comes by, threatening to take the life of an old countryman (ku) unless the latter agrees to "pay back" a trumped up debt of two hundred coppers. Chao intervenes and, with reluctance, bails the old man out by offering all he has. When the news reaches his wife, she is exasperated.

Act III

The ku, named Chang T'ien-chüeh, happens to be a high official in disguise. He sends Chao ten gold phoenix hairpins in return for his favor. Chao gives the Innkeeper one hairpin as payment for his room and board and buries the others behind the door. Meanwhile, Tiger Li has murdered a servant of the powerful Yang family and gotten away with ten silver spoons. Taking lodging at the same inn as the Chaos', he discovers the gold hair ornaments, leaves his spoons in their stead, and flees.

Yang and his men come to search and find the scholar with the spoons. Tortured beyond endurance, Chao admits to the murder charge.

Act IV

Tiger Li goes to a silversmith to exchange the nine hairpins for cash. When the Innkeeper does the same with his lone hairpin, he discovers that Tiger Li is the true culprit. He waits for the bully's reappearance and, with the help of the silversmith and others, captures Tiger Li and takes him to the judges, who then pronounce judgment and restore justice.

NOTES
(For full citations see Bibliography)

Chapter I

1. Lo Chin-t'ang's 羅錦堂 classification has ten tsa-chü under the
   heading of "chüeh-yi p'ing-fan," or "determining the doubtful case
   and reversing the judgment." Here I have appropriated the phrase
   p'ing-fan without following Lo's classification, which seems inconsistent and a bit arbitrary. See Lo, pp. 427-428, 433.

2. Hayden (I). See also Hayden (II).

3. In his discussion of the courtroom plays, Hayden deals with twenty-
   six plays altogether. See Hayden (I).

4. Throughout this study, I have used the terms Yüan tsa-chü, Yüan
   drama, and Yüan plays interchangeably. Unless otherwise stated,
   they all refer to the kind of drama produced in Yüan (and early
   Ming) times commonly known as pei tsa-chü 北雜劇, or "northern tsa-chü plays."

5. Lo, "Preface," p. ii. Hsü T'iao-fu's Registry of Extant Yüan
   Plays, which includes plays "written in the Yüan-Ming transitional
   period," has more than two hundred titles. See Hsü T'iao-fu.
   For the view of another scholar, see Fu.

6. Scenarios for all seven plays can be found in the Appendix.

7. The question of authorship of many plays is moot and lies outside
   the boundary of this study; the attribution here follows Lo Chin-
   t'ang's. See Lo.

8. Also called Pu-jen-shih 不認屍 or Refusing the Corpse, which
   Yen Tun-yi 嚴敦易 claims to be a more appropriate title. See
   Yen, p. 753.

162

9. Also called <u>Shih t'an-tzu</u> 十探子 or <u>The Ten Deputies</u>.

10. See, for instance, Hawkes, pp. 78-79.

11. It should be noted that the Chinese detective story predates its Western counterpart by approximately six hundred years.

12. Chou Te-ch'ing.

13. I refer to its subtitle: 正語之本, 變雅之端"<u>Cheng-yü chih pen,
pien-ya chih tuan</u>." Chou Te-ch'ing, p. 183.

14. Yen-nan chih-an [pseud.]

15. Yen-nan chih-an [pseud.], pp. 160-61. Shih Chung-wen, however, believes that "the overall effect created by a certain music mode in one act can still be significant" despite occasional "inconsistency between the music and words in certain scenes." See Shih (I), p. 30. Dale Johnson's latest work takes serious exception to such views, however.

16. Chu Ch'üan.

17. Ibid., p. 16. Cf. also Aoki Masaru's comments in Aoki, p. 62.

18. Wang Chi-te.

19. Ibid., p. 141.

20. Shen.

21. Ibid., p. 214.

22. See his second preface to <u>YCH</u>. For a discussion of this theory, see Crump (I), pp. 43-44, 45.

23. Wang Chi-te, p. 148

24. On the other hand, this may explain in part the dominance of lyricism in classical Chinese drama.

Chapter I Notes

25. In his own words: "Usually it turned out that I had barely finished a play when the producer would grab it away. Sometimes the second half of the script was not yet written when the first half was already mounted on stage."--Li Yü, p. 58.

26. Li Yü.

27. Whether he was a successful or even faithful practitioner of his own theory is of course an entirely different matter.

28. Ibid., pp. 22 and 26.

29. In Wang Kuo-wei, pp. 199-226 and pp. 149-97, respectively.

30. Ibid., pp. 1-148.

31. This, along with Ch'ü lu 曲錄, is the basis for serious research of Yüan drama in the early years of the Republic. Cf. Cheng Chen-to, p. 631.

32. Ibid., p. 3.

33. Ibid., p. 105.

34. Ibid., p. 106.

35. Ibid., p. 110.

36. Wang Kuo-wei, p. 106.

37. Cheng Ch'ien (I), 12.

38. See under Cheng Ch'ien.

39. Hu Shih, chüan 4.

40. Ibid.

41. Ibid.

Chapter I Notes

42. Li K'ai-Hsien.

43. Ibid., p. 298.

44. Cf. West.

45. Hsieh.

46. Ibid., p. 32.

47. The Chinese reads, 借文字作革命事業 . Ibid., p. 28.

48. Cheng Chen-to, pp. 516-17.

49. Chu Tung-jun (I) and (II).

50. Ibid., (II), p. 18.

51. Ibid., (I), p. 15.

52. <u>YMC</u>.

53. Hsü Shuo-fang, p. 27.

54. Paul H. Ch'en believes that the Yüan laws show more leniency than the statutes of many other dynasties in China. See Ch'en.

55. Li Tze-fen.

56. Wang Chi-ssu (I), p. 131. But in an earlier article, Wang criticized the ending of the play for being as weak as "a spent arrow." See Wang Chi-ssu (II), p. 143.

57. For example: "I do not consider it an exaggeration to state that Yüan drama is a mirror of the Chinese society in Yüan times. In Yüan drama, we can see the complete picture of people's life of the time."--Sung, p. 3.

58. Aoki.

59. See, for instance, Crump (I), pp. 54-56.

Chapter I Notes

60. Yoshikawa.

61. Iwaki.

62. Among his published translations of Yüan drama are: "Li K'uei
    Carries Thorns," in Anthology of Chinese Literature: From Early
    Times to the Fourteenth Century, ed. Cyril Birch (New York:
    Grove Press Inc., 1965), pp. 393-421; "Rain on the Hsiao-hsiang,"
    Renditions 4 (Spring 1975): 49-70. "The Mo-ho-lo Doll" is appen-
    ded to the forthcoming book, Crump (VI).

63. See under Crump.

64. Johnson.

65. Shih (II).

66. Wang Kuo-wei, p. 106.

67. Ch'ien, 37.

68. Liu.

69. Published by National Taiwan University.

70. Cheng Ch'ien (II).

71. Cf. Hawkes, pp. 80-81.

72. Sun K'ai-ti, especially pp. 151-52. Sun's view is shared by Cheng
    Ch'ien; see also Cheng Ch'ien (I) and (III).

73. Sun K'ai-ti suggests that all Ming editions of Yüan drama are in
    one way or another related to the nei-fu pen 內府本 or "court
    edition"; he maintains, however, that these editions (excepting
    YCH) are still close to the original Yüan text. (See Sun K'ai-ti,
    pp. 152, 153.) David Hawkes, drawing on the findings of Yoshikawa
    and Iwaki, comes to the conclusion that "the responsibility for the
    difference [between the dialogue in the Ming texts and that of the
    Yüan originals] rests not so much with the sixteenth and seven-
    teenth century editors, as with the Ming court players of a century
    or two earlier." (Hawkes, p. 79.)

Chapter I Notes

74. Sui.

Chapter II Notes

1. Except where noted (at the end of each quoted passage), translations are mine.

2. "Reflecting" for the character 映. See Cavanaugh, p. 106.

3. Cavanaugh, p. 65. On p. 63, Cavanaugh states: "I concur wholeheartedly in the general consensus of opinion that [Rain] is Pai P'u's masterpiece and one of the finest Yüan plays. [It] achieves this distinction, however, not through the scope and power of its drama but solely through the beautiful lyricism of its poetry . . . ."

4. With a few minor changes (in square brackets), I have used Donald Keene's translation. Keene, p. 442.

5. Keene, p. 443.

6. The term is borrowed from criticism of fiction. See Wellek and Warren, pp. 218-19.

7. In YCH and WP the term tz'u must be understood to mean simply "rhymed and rhythmic verses"; they almost never resemble the Sung dynasty "lyric" in form. For a discussion of these "theater poems" see Martin, pp. 248-58.

8. See Crump (IV), p. 27.

9. Crump (IV), p. 27. Richard F. S. Yang suggests that some of the entering or exit pieces "are meant to create a dramatic and artistic atmosphere and to put the audience in communication with the players"--because these pieces are "common sayings." See Yang, pp. 184-86.

10. A modern English version of this play exists in Liu Jung-en's Six Yüan Plays, but the passages quoted here are my translations because Liu has, in his own words, "omitted passages in dialogue

Chapter II Notes

and in verse which are obscure . . . . inessential to the play as a whole, or tiresomely repetitive." (sic) (Liu Jung-en, p. 20.)

11. Professor Crump's translation. Crump (III), p. 475.

12. Crump (III), p. 474.

13. Crump (III), p. 475.

14. Crump (III), pp. 475-76.

15. Crump (VI).

16. Almost all judgment reversal plays poke fun at the obtuse, incompetent, and/or venal officials; some of the jokes are identical. Cf., for instance, The Child Shen-nu-erh (YCH, p. 568) and Rescue of the Filial Son (YCH, p. 767). Stephen West believes, with Tanaka Kenji, that these are some of the stock scenes that had their origins in the Chin Dynasty yüan-pen 院本. See Tanaka, p. 178 ff. and West.

17. Crump (VI).

18. Cf. Aristotle's discussion on the excellence of poetic expression in Poetics, p. 59. See also Yang, p. 190.

19. Shih (I), p. 23.

20. Shih (I), pp. 74-77.

21. Shih (I), pp. 188-93.

22. Shih (I), pp. 22-23.

23. Both of them are missed by Shih Chung-wen in her translation, probably because the great number of padding words and apostrophies obscure the meter and call attention away from the rhyme.

24. Shih (I), p. 59.

25. Shih (I), p. 65.

Chapter II Notes

26. Cf., for instance, the Examination Official in Rain on the Hsiao-
hsiang (潇湘雨 Hsiao-hsiang-yü), YCH, pp. 250-51; Crump
(VII), pp. 55-56. See also Tanaka and West.

27. Yen Tun-yi argues that the play should be more appropriately
called Pu-jen-shih 不認屍 (Refusing the Corpse). Yen, p. 753.

28. Chang Ch'ien 張千 is a conventional appellation for any male servant or low-ranking clerk in Yüan drama, despite W. L. Idema's
claim that Chang Ch'ien is explicitly "the main yamen clerk and an
official's servant." See Idema, 345.

29. In The Chalk Circle, after his Solomon's Judgment has discovered
the truth of a legal case, Judge Pao also declares that "although
the intention of the law is now obscure, it can still be inferred by
observing human feelings . . . ." (YCH, p. 1128), and his speech
relates to the drama.

30. Aoki notes that Mrs. Yang "looks as though she were an attorney"
throughout the legal proceedings. Aoki, p. 87.

31. Ethel Van Der Veer's translation is not usable because of its many
mistakes. Its "politeness" does not help my thesis in this section,
either. She also erroneously attributed the play to that prolific
composer, Anon. See Van Der Veer.

32. Crump (VI).

33. For a speculation of the origin of this sobriquet, see Hayden (II),
p. 267.

34. The editor of YCH attributes the play to Sun Chung-chang 孫仲章 ,
but see Yen, pp. 322-27, and Lo, pp. 61-62.

35. The term ch'ou 丑 is probably a Ming dynasty invention. See
Cheng Chen-to, p. 563.

36. For the formation of A-Ch'en's name, see Hayden (II), p. 235,
note 5.

Chapter III Notes

1. Shih (II), pp. 45-51.

2. Wells, p. 114.

3. Wells, pp. 114-19.

4. Styan, p. 175.

5. Doran, p. 234.

6. Doran, p. 232; Styan, p. 170.

7. Shih (I), pp. 155-61.

8. Crump (VI).

9. Cf. Tanaka, p. 178ff. and West.

10. Hayden (II), pp. 247-49.

11. Bribing is alluded to in all judgment reversal plays except Hair-pins: Child, YCH, p. 568; Kerchief, YCH, p. 681; Rescue, YCH, p. 767; Circle, YCH, p. 1116; Doll, YCH, p. 1375; and Injustice, YCH, p. 1507. It actually takes place on stage in Child (YCH, p. 571) and Doll (YCH, p. 1376).

12. George A. Hayden believes that Judge Pao errs in reading the outcome of the chalk circle experiment (Hayden [I], p. 212), but I interpret it as a ploy to get the true mother to spell out her own reason for not dragging the child--apparently a dramatic consideration. As evidence, consider the fact that even before the Chalk Circle is drawn, Pao has already sent for Mrs. Ma's paramour.

13. Hayden (I), pp. 211-13.

14. Chang, p. 135.

15. Josephine Huang Hung takes brief note of the fact that Tou Ngo "is no saint," that "she is not devoid of all human desires--of joy and even of the desire for the opposite sex." See Hung, p. 45.

170

Chapter III Notes

16. Chang, pp. 128-41.

17. Generally, I have followed Professor Shih Chung-wen's translation of Injustice. When it is strictly adhered to, the note says simply "Shih (I)," followed by pagination. When minor alterations are made to bring out my point, the note reads "based on Shih (I)," with pagination. There are also cases when I attempted my own translation, to which there is no note.

18. Based on Shih (I), pp. 61-63.

19. Shih (I), pp. 73-75.

20. Based on Shih (I), pp. 75-79.

21. Cf. Hsü Wen-tou, pp. 109-10.

22. Based on Shih (I), pp. 92-101.

23. Based on Shih (I), pp. 130-39.

24. The note provided by Shih says: "'catching a phoenix' or 'trapping a dragon' is usually interpreted as 'to hurt a good person'" (Shih [II], p. 135). But the context seems to me to favor a different interpretation, namely, "extramarital adventures," dragon and phoenix being common metaphors for male and female, respectively.

25. Based on Shih (I), pp. 177-81.

26. Based on Shih (I), pp. 78-83.

27. Crump (VI).

28. Ibid.

29. It is significant that the composer seems to have consciously cast Kao Shan as a wai 外 --a less rowdy and boisterous, more refined, comic character than a ching 淨 or ch'ou 丑. Feng Ming-hui 馮明惠 in a recent article also noted that Kao Shan is a success as a character (Feng, pp. 138-40).

Chapter III Notes

30. Crump (VI).

31. Ibid.

32. Ibid.

33. Ibid.

34. Ibid.

35. Ibid.

36. Ibid.

37. Ibid.

38. Ibid.

39. Ibid.

40. Ibid.

41. Ibid.

Chapter IV Notes

1. Professors Cheng Ch'ien and Dale Johnson have done commendable jobs in this area. See under Cheng Ch'ien and Johnson.

2. The most recent and most comprehensive effort in this respect is Professor J. I. Crump's forthcoming book, Chinese Theater in the Days of Kublai Khan.

3. Most recently, Chung-wai wen-hsueh (Taipei: National Taiwan University) has published a series of "Modern Views on Yüan Tsa-chü." Although some of these articles tend to impose modern Western standards on the medieval Chinese theater, they reflect respectable scholarly interest and effort in the direction of viewing tsa-chü as drama.

A SELECT BIBLIOGRAPHY

Aoki, Masaru 青木正兒. <u>Gennin zatsugeki josetsu</u> 元人雜劇序説.
Chinese translation by Sui Shu-sen 隋樹森, revised and augmented by Hsü T'iao-fu 徐調孚. Hongkong: Chien-wen shu-chü, 1959.

Aristotle. <u>Poetics</u>. Translated with an Introduction by Gerald F. Else. Ann Arbor: The University of Michigan Press, 1967.

Cavanaugh, J. "The Dramatic Works of the Yüan Dynasty Playwright Pai P'u." Ph.D. dissertation, Stanford University, 1975.

Chang, Han-liang 張漢良. "Kuan Han-ch'ing te Tou Ngo yüan: yi-ke t'ung-su-chü" 關漢卿的竇娥冤: 一個通俗劇. <u>Chung-wai wen-hsüeh</u> 中外文學 (National Taiwan University) 4(1976): 128-41.

Yen-nan Chih-an [pseud.] 燕南芝庵. <u>Ch'ang lun</u> 唱論. <u>Chung-kuo ku-tien hsi-ch'ü lun-chu chi-ch'eng</u> (KTHC) 1(1959): 153-66.

Ch'en, Paul H. "Chinese Legal Tradition in the Yüan Period." A paper presented to the ACLS Conference on the Impact of Mongul Rule on Chinese Civilization, Maine, July 1976.

Cheng, Chen-to 鄭振鐸. <u>Chung-kuo wen-hsüeh yen-chiu</u> 中國文學研究. 3 vols. Peking: Tso-chia ch'u-pan-she, 1957.

Cheng, Ch'ien 鄭騫. (I) "Tsang Mao-hsün kai-ting Yüan tsa-chü p'ing-yi" 臧懋循改訂元雜劇平議. <u>Wen-shih-che hsüeh-pao</u> 文史哲學報 (National Taiwan University) 10(1961): 1-13.

_____. (II) <u>Chiao-ting Yüan-k'an tsa-chü san-shih chung</u> 校訂元刊雜劇三十種. Taipei: Shih-chieh shu-chü, 1962.

_____. (III) "Yüan-Ming ch'ao-k'e Yüan-jen tsa-chü chiu-chung t'i-yao" 元明鈔刻元人雜劇九種提要. <u>Tsing-hua Journal of Chinese Studies</u>, new series, 7(1969): 145-55.

_____. (IV) <u>Pei-ch'ü hsin-p'u</u> 北曲新譜. Taipei: Yi-wen ch'u-pan-she, 1973.

173

_____. (V) Ts'ung shih tao ch'ü 從詩到曲. Taipei: K'o-hsüeh ch'u-pan-she, 1961.

_____. (VI) "Yüan-jen tsa-chü te chieh-kou" 元人雜劇的結構. Ta-lu tsa-chih 大陸雜誌 2(1951).

Ch'ien, Chung-shu 錢鐘書. "Tragedy in Old Chinese Drama." T'ien Hsia Monthly 1(1935): 37-46.

Chou, Te-ch'ing 周德清. Chung-yüan yin-yün 中原音韻. KTHC 1(1959): 167-285.

Chu, Ch'üan 朱權. T'ai-ho cheng-yin p'u 太和正音譜. KTHC 3(1959): 1-231.

Chu, Tung-jun 朱東潤. (I) "Yüan tsa-chü chi ch'i shih-tai" 元雜劇及其時代 (Part 1). Kuo-wen yüeh-k'an 國文月刊 77(1949): 12-18.

_____. (II) "Yüan tsa-chü chi ch'i shih-tai" (Part 2). Kuo-wen yüeh-k'an 78(1949): 12-18.

Chung-kuo ku-tien hsi-ch'ü lun-chu chi-ch'eng 中國古典戲劇論著集成. 10 vols. Peking: Chung-kuo hsi-chü ch'u-pan-she, 1959.

Chung-wen ta-tz'u-tien 中文大辭典. Taipei: The Institute for Advanced Chinese Studies, College of Chinese Culture, 1968.

Crump, J. I. (I) "Giants in the Earth: Yüan Drama as Seen by Ming Critics." Tamkang Review 5(1974): 33-62.

_____. (II) "The Elements of Yüan Opera." The Journal of Asian Studies 17(1958): 417-34.

_____. (III) "Yüan-pen, Yüan Drama's Rowdy Ancestor." Literature East & West 14(1970): 473-90.

_____. (IV) "The Conventions and Craft of Yüan Drama." Journal of the American Oriental Society 91(1971): 14-29.

_____. (V) "Spoken Verse in Yüan Drama." Tamkang Review 4(1973): 41-52.

175

_____. (VI) <u>Chinese Theater in the Days of Kublai Khan</u>. Tucson: University of Arizona Press, forthcoming.

_____. (VII) "Rain on the Hsiao-hsiang." <u>Renditions</u> 4(1975): 49-70.

_____. (VIII) <u>Chinese and Japanese Music Dramas</u>. Michigan Papers in Chinese Studies, vol. 19. Ann Arbor: University of Michigan, Center for Chinese Studies, 1975.

Doran, Madeleine. <u>Endeavors of Art: A Study of Form in Elizabethan Drama</u>. Madison: The University of Wisconsin Press, 1954.

Feng, Ming-hui 馮明惠. "<u>Mo-ho-lo</u> tsa-chü te hsin-shang" 魔合羅雜劇的欣賞. <u>Chung-wai wen-hsüeh</u> 4(1976): 124-42.

Fu, Hsi-hua 傅惜華. <u>Yüan-jen tsa-chü ch'üan-mu</u> 元人雜劇全目. Peking: Tso-chia ch'u-pan-she, 1957.

Hawkes, David. "Reflections on Some Yüan Tsa-chü." <u>Asia Major</u> 16(1971): 14-29.

Hayden, George A. (I) "The Courtroom Plays of the Yüan and Early Ming Periods." <u>Harvard Journal of Asiatic Studies</u> 34(1974): 192-220.

_____. (II) "The Judge Pao Plays of the Yüan Dynasty." Ph.D. dissertation, Stanford University, 1971.

Hsieh, Wan-ying 謝婉瑩. "Yüan-tai te hsi-chü" 元代的戲劇. <u>Yen-ching hsüeh-pao</u> 燕京學報 1(1927): 15-51.

Hsü, Shuo-fang 徐朔方. <u>Hsi-ch'ü tsa-chi</u> 戲曲雜記. Shanghai: Ku-tien wen-hsüeh ch'u-pan-she, 1956.

Hsü, T'iao-fu 徐調孚. <u>Hsien-ts'un Yüan-jen tsa-chü shu-lu</u> 現存元人雜劇書錄. Shanghai: Ku-tien wen-hsüeh ch'u-pan-she, 1957.

Hsü, Wen-tou 徐文斗. "Kuan Han-ch'ing chü-tso chung te fu-nü hsing-hsiang" 關漢卿劇作中的婦女形象. <u>Yüan-Ming-Ch'ing hsi-ch'ü lun-wen-chi</u> (YMC) 2(1959): 99-122.

Hu, Shih 胡侍. Chen-chu ch'uan 真珠船, in Kuan-chung ts'ung-shu 關中叢書. Shansi: Shansi t'ung-chih-kuan, 1934-36.

Huang, Wen-yang 黃文暘. Ch'ü-hai 曲海. Compiled in 1777-81.

Hung, Josephine Huang. "Kuan Han-ch'ing and His Sorrows of Toh O." Asian Culture Quarterly (Taipei) 4(1976): 36-47.

Idema, W. L. "Review of Chung-wen Shih's Injustice to Tou O." T'oung Pao 60(1974): 344-47.

Iwaki, Hideo 岩城秀夫. Chūgoku gikyoku engeki kenkyū 中國戲曲 演劇研究. Tokyo: Sobunsha, 1972.

Johnson, Dale. "The Prosody of Yüan Drama." T'oung Pao 56(1970): 96-146.

Keene, Donald, trans. "Autumn in the Palace of Han." In Anthology of Chinese Literature from Early Times to the Fourteenth Century, edited by Cyril Birch. New York: Grove Press, Inc., 1965.

Legge, James, trans. The Chinese Classics.

Li, K'ai-hsien. Li K'ai-hsien chi 李開先集. Edited by Lu Kung 路工. 3 vols. Peking: Tso-chia ch'u-pan-she, 1957.

Li, Tze-fen 李則芬. (I) "Meng-ku yang-kao-erh-li yü Yüan ch'u wo-t'o-ch'ien chih yen-chiu" 蒙古羊羔兒利與元初斡脫錢 之研究 (Part 1). Tung-fang tsa-chih 東方雜誌 7(1974): 29-33.

_____. (II) "Meng-ku yang-kao-erh-li yü Yüan-ch'u wo-t'o-ch'ien chih yen-chiu" (Part 2). Tung-fang tsa-chih 7(1974): 44-47.

Li, Yü 李漁. Hsien-ch'ing ou-chi 閒情偶記. KTHC 7(1959): 1-114.

Liu, James J. H. "Elizabethan and Yüan." London: China Society, 1955.

Liu, Jung-en, trans. Six Yüan Plays, with an Introduction. Middlesex, England: Penguin Books, 1972.

Lo, Chin-t'ang 羅錦堂. Hsien-ts'un yüan-jen tsa-chü pen-shih k'ao 現存元人雜劇本事考. Taipei: Chung-kuo wen-hua-shih-yeh, 1960.

Martin, Helmut. "Lyricism in Yuan Drama." Études d'histoire et de literature chinoises (Bibliotheque de l'institut des hautes études chinoises) 24(1976): 248-58.

Shen, Te-fu 沈德符. Ku-ch'ü tsa-yen 顧曲雜言. KTHC 4(1959): 193-228.

Shih, Chung-wen. (I) Injustice to Tou O (Tou O yüan), a study and translation. Cambridge, England: Cambridge University Press, 1972.

_____. (II) The Golden Age of Chinese Drama: Yüan Tsa-chü. Princeton: Princeton University Press, 1976.

Styan, J. L. The Elements of Drama. Cambridge, England: Cambridge University Press, 1960.

Sui, Shu-sen 隋樹森, ed. Yüan-ch'ü hsüan wai-pien [WP] 元曲選 外編. 3 vols. Peking: Chung-hua shu-chü, 1959. Reprint in Taipei: Chung-hua shu-chü, 1967.

Sun, K'ai-ti 孫楷第. Yeh-shih-yüan ku-chin tsa-chü k'ao 也是園 古今雜劇考. Shanghai: Shang-tsa ch'u-pan-she, 1953.

Sung, Han-cho 宋漢濯. "Yüan-chü te hsien-shih chu-yi ching-shen" 元劇的現實主義精神. YMC 2(1959): 1-19.

Tanaka, Kenji 田中謙二. "Genbun kō" 院本考. The Nippon-Chūgoku-Gakkai-ho 20(1970): 169-91.

Tsang, Mao-hsün 臧懋循, ed. Yüan-ch'ü hsüan 元曲選. Taipei: Cheng-wen shu-chü, 1970.

Van Der Veer, Ethel, trans. "The Chalk Circle." In World Drama, edited by Barrett H. Clark. New York: Dover Publications Inc., 1933.

Wang, Chi-ssu 王季思. (I) "T'an Kuan Han-ch'ing te Lu Chai-lang tsa-chü" 談關漢卿的魯齋郎雜劇. YMC 2(1959): 131-47.

_____. (II) "Kuan Han-ch'ing he t'a-te tsa-chü" 關漢卿和他 的雜劇. Ku-tien wen-hsüeh yen-chiu hui-k'an 古典文學研 究彙刊, vol. 1. Shanghai: Ku-tien wen-hsüeh ch'u-pan-she, 1955.

178

—————— (III) "Yüan-chü chung hsieh-yin shuang-kuan-yü" 元劇中諧
音雙關語. Kuo-wen yüeh-k'an 67(1948): 15-19.

Wang, Chi-te 王驥德. Ch'ü lü 曲律. KTHC 4(1959): 43-191.

Wang, Kuo-wei 王國維. Wang Kuo-wei hsi-ch'ü lun-wen-chi 王國維
戲曲論文集. Peking: Chung-kuo hsi-chü ch'u-pan-she,
1959.

Wellek, Rene and Warren, Austin. Theory of Literature. Middlesex,
England: Penguin Books, 1968.

Wells, Henry W. The Classical Drama of the Orient. New York: Asia
Publishing House, 1965.

West, Stephen H. "Mongol Influence on the Development of Northern
Drama." A paper presented to the ACLS Conference on the Impact
of Mongol Rule on Chinese Civilization, Maine, July 1976.

Yang, Richard F. S. "The Function of Poetry in the Yüan Drama."
Monumenta Serica 29(1970-71): 163-92.

Yen, Tun-yi 嚴敦易. Yüan-chü chen-yi 元劇斟疑. 2 vols. Peking:
Chung-hua shu-chü, 1960.

Yoshikawa, Kōjirō 吉川幸次郎. Gen zatsugeki kenkyū 元雜劇研
究. Chinese translation by Cheng Ch'ing-mao 鄭清茂. Taipei:
Yi-wen, 1960.

Yüan-ch'ü hsüan. See under Tsang.

Yüan-ch'ü hsüan wai-pien. See under Sui.

Yüan-Ming-Ch'ing hsi-ch'ü lun-wen-chi 元明戲曲論文集戲,
vol. 2. Peking: Jen-min wen-hsüeh ch'u-pan-she, 1959.

MICHIGAN PAPERS IN CHINESE STUDIES

No. 2. The Cultural Revolution: 1967 in Review, four essays by Michel Oksenberg, Carl Riskin, Robert Scalapino, and Ezra Vogel.

No. 3. Two Studies in Chinese Literature, by Li Chi and Dale Johnson.

No. 4. Early Communist China: Two Studies, by Ronald Suleski and Daniel Bays.

No. 5. The Chinese Economy, ca. 1870-1911, by Albert Feuerwerker.

No. 6. Chinese Paintings in Chinese Publications, 1956-1968: An Annotated Bibliography and an Index to the Paintings, by E. J. Laing.

No. 7. The Treaty Ports and China's Modernization: What Went Wrong? by Rhoads Murphey.

No. 8. Two Twelfth Century Texts on Chinese Painting, by Robert J. Maeda.

No. 9. The Economy of Communist China, 1949-1969, by Chu-yuan Cheng.

No. 10. Educated Youth and the Cultural Revolution in China, by Martin Singer.

No. 11. Premodern China: A Bibliographical Introduction, by Chun-shu Chang.

No. 12. Two Studies on Ming History, by Charles O. Hucker.

No. 13. Nineteenth Century China: Five Imperialist Perspectives, selected by Dilip Basu, edited by Rhoads Murphey.

No. 14. Modern China, 1840-1972: An Introduction to Sources and Research Aids, by Andrew J. Nathan.

No. 15. Women in China: Studies in Social Change and Feminism, edited by Marilyn B. Young.

No. 16. An Annotated Bibliography of Chinese Painting Catalogues and Related Texts, by Hin-cheung Lovell.

No. 17. China's Allocation of Fixed Capital Investment, 1952-1957, by Chu-yuan Cheng.

No. 18. Health, Conflict, and the Chinese Political System, by David M. Lampton.

No. 19. Chinese and Japanese Music-Dramas, edited by J. I. Crump and William P. Malm.

MICHIGAN ABSTRACTS OF CHINESE AND
JAPANESE WORKS ON CHINESE HISTORY

No. 1. The Ming Tribute Grain System, by Hoshi Ayao, translated by Mark Elvin.

No. 2. Commerce and Society in Sung China, by Shiba Yoshinobu, translated by Mark Elvin.

No. 3. Transport in Transition: The Evolution of Traditional Shipping in China, translations by Andrew Watson.

No. 4. Japanese Perspectives on China's Early Modernization: A Bibliographical Survey, by K. H. Kim.

No. 5. The Silk Industry in Ch'ing China, by Shih Min-hsiung, translated by E-tu Zen Sun.

NONSERIES PUBLICATION

Index to the "Chan-kuo Ts'e," by Sharon Fidler and J. I. Crump. A companion volume to the Chan-kuo Ts'e, translated by J. I. Crump (Oxford: Clarendon Press, 1970).

Michigan Papers and Abstracts available from:

Center for Chinese Studies
The University of Michigan
Lane Hall (Publications)
Ann Arbor, MI 48109 USA

Prepaid Orders Only
write for complete price listing

Printed and bound by CPI Group (UK) Ltd, Croydon, CR0 4YY

13/04/2025

14656508-0001